HOGARTH LECTURES ON LITERATURE

STUDIES IN SHAKESPEARE

Hogarth Lectures on Literature Series

Editors: GEORGE RYLANDS and LEONARD WOOLF

1. (*Introductory Volume*) A LECTURE ON LECTURES *by* SIR ARTHUR QUILLER-COUCH ("Q"), Professor of English Literature, Cambridge University.
2. TRAGEDY *by* F. L. LUCAS, Fellow of King's College, Cambridge.
3. STUDIES IN SHAKESPEARE *by* ALLARDYCE NICOLL, Professor of English Language and Literature in the University of London.
4. THE DEVELOPMENT OF ENGLISH BIOGRAPHY *by* HAROLD NICOLSON.

In Preparation

DEVELOPMENT OF THE 19TH CENTURY LYRIC *by* H. J. C. GRIERSON, Professor of English Literature, Edinburgh University.

THE HISTORICAL NOVEL *by* HUGH WALPOLE.

PHASES OF FICTION *by* VIRGINIA WOOLF.

PLOT IN THE NOVEL *by* EDWIN MUIR.

THE DEVELOPMENT OF ENGLISH BIOGRAPHY

BY
HAROLD NICOLSON

NEW YORK
HARCOURT, BRACE AND COMPANY

COPYRIGHT, 1928, BY
HARCOURT, BRACE AND COMPANY, INC.

PRINTED IN THE U. S. A. BY
QUINN & BODEN COMPANY, INC.
RAHWAY, N. J.

CONTENTS

LECTURE		PAGE
I.	ORIGINS OF ENGLISH BIOGRAPHY, A.D. 500-1599	7
II.	THE SEVENTEENTH CENTURY, 1599-1667	38
III.	FROM WALTON TO JOHNSON, 1670-1780	64
IV.	THE BOSWELL FORMULA, 1791	87
V.	THE NINETEENTH CENTURY	109
VI.	THE PRESENT AGE	132

THE DEVELOPMENT OF ENGLISH BIOGRAPHY

I

ORIGINS OF ENGLISH BIOGRAPHY, A.D. 500-1599

Definition of biography—"Pure" and "impure" biography—Dangers of exaggerated reverence, didacticism, or subjectivity—Importance of truth and construction—Relation of "pure" biography to memoirs, letters, journals, and autobiography—Origins of English biography—Runic inscriptions—Sagas, elegies, hagiography—Bede—Asser's *Life of Alfred*—The chronicles—Eadmer's *Vita Anselmi*—The revival of curiosity—William of Malmesbury—Geoffrey of Monmouth—Matthew Paris—The age of romance—Chaucer—The fifteenth century—The sixteenth century—The Tudor chronicles—Hall—Holinshed—John Leland—Foxe's martyrology—North's *Plutarch*—*The History of Richard III*—Sir John Hayward—Roper's *More*—Cavendish's *Wolsey*—Biography in 1599.

THE Oxford Dictionary defines biography as "the history of the lives of individual men as a branch of literature." This definition is convenient: it insists on three essential elements—"history," "individual," and "literature";

Definition of biography.

it prescribes by implication that biography must be a truthful record of an individual and composed as a work of art; it thus excludes narratives which are unhistorical, which do not deal primarily with individuals, or which are not composed with a conscious artistic purpose. Such exclusion is important. It is clearly useless to trace the development of the art of biography in English literature unless we are first quite clear what works should be included in, or excluded from, this elastic category. It is not sufficient merely to differentiate biography from history on the one hand and fiction on the other: we must try to give it a more precise location; we must endeavour to find some formula which will place it in the proper relation to such cognate modes of expression as journals, diaries, memoirs, imaginary portraits, or mere jottings of gossip and conversation; we must above all distinguish "pure" from "impure" biography; and having thus narrowed down the art of biography to a recognisable and distinct form of narrative, we must indicate what elements go to render any particular biography either "good" or "bad."

The biographies written and published in this country are innumerable. In selecting those which I desire to bring to your notice, I am conscious that

ORIGINS OF ENGLISH BIOGRAPHY

I am undertaking the invidious task of the anthologist, and that my inclusions or omissions will clash with individual predilections. But my selections are not entirely empirical; I shall be governed in the first place by a constant desire to differentiate "pure" from "impure" biography, and in the second place I shall endeavour to treat in detail only such works as you have read, or can conveniently read, for yourselves.

Let me at the outset define what, in my opinion, are the elements which constitute a "pure" biography. In tracing the development of this art in England, I shall show how seldom it was properly differentiated or isolated; how frequently its outlines were confused by elements extraneous to the art itself. Predominant among these confusing elements was the desire to celebrate the dead—a desire wholly distinct from, and generally inimical to, the actual art of biography, but which can be traced as the main factor in "impure" biography from the old runic inscriptions, through the hagiographers, past the funeral orations of Jeremy Taylor to such absurd Victorian apotheoses as Lady Burton's *Life* of her brilliant and erratic husband. A second, and almost equally pregnant, cause of "impure" biography is the desire to compose the life of an individual as an

"Pure" and "impure" biography.

illustration of some extraneous theory or conception. Here again the hagiographers are much to blame; but the system is as old as Suetonius, and has been used ever since by theologians, moralists, cranks, and politicians. A third cause of "impure" biography is undue subjectivity in the writer. To a certain extent a subjective attitude is desirable and inevitable; and indeed the most perfect of English biographies, such as Lockhart's *Life of Scott*, inevitably contain or convey a sketch of the biographer subsidiary to that of the central portrait. The undue intrusion of the biographer's personality or predilections is, however, a constant source of impurity; it has spoilt many a good biography, as, for instance, Walton's *Lives*, which are marred throughout by the author's desire to give to all his characters, even to the tortured and tormented Donne, the same qualities of scholarly and devout complacency as he possessed, and valued, in himself.

Such then are the main causes of "impure" biography—either an undue desire to celebrate the dead, or a purpose extraneous to the work itself, or an undue subjectivity on the part of the biographer. The essentials of "pure" biography are the reverse of the above. The primary essential is that of historical truth, by which is meant not merely the avoidance of misstatements, but the wider veracity of complete and accurate portraiture. The suppression or evasion of absolute truth is in fact the common error of biographers, who seek to palliate their deficiency by an appeal to irrelevant considerations such as "loyalty," "reverence," and "discretion." Obviously all malice or all unnecessary infliction of pain must be avoided by the biographer. But should he feel that he can draw no truthful picture of his victim without wounding the feelings of survivors or the morals of his age, then assuredly he should not sully his conscience by the suggestion of untruth but rather abandon his project, and wait until the passage of time shall render his disclosures less scandalous or painful. This lack of truth in English biography is, as it happens, largely traditional, and is caused by accidents in the history of its development which will be noted and explained in succeeding lectures. In the nineteenth century, however, this accidental tradition was given the authority of a moral law. "The history of mankind," wrote Carlyle, "is the history of its great men: to find out these, clean the dirt from them, and place them on their proper pedestal." So late as 1896 Sir Sidney Lee could define the inspiration of biography as "an instinctive desire to do honour to the memories of those who, by character and exploits, have distinguished themselves from the mass of their countrymen."[1] Conversely, the Victorians missed no opportunity to brand as "cruel and vulgar" any attempt at honest biography: Froude fell into the darkest disgrace over his recollections of Carlyle; and even Lord Houghton's harmless work on Keats aroused Lord Tennyson to a bellow of indignation.

Such exaggerated regard for reverence and caution has produced endless commemorative volumes; it has also ruined several biographies. It proceeds predominantly from the habit of regarding biography as something other than a record of personality. Were biography generally accepted as an important branch of psychology, the high standards inherent in that science would impose their own discipline and sanctions. "White-washing" would be considered as nefarious as malignity; inaccuracy of representation as more culpable even than inaccuracy of fact: a "bad" biography would pass as unnoticed as a feeble novel; and this ideal of scientific honesty would free biography from the entanglements by which it is at present obstructed and obscured.

The second essential of pure biography is that it shall be well constructed. I do not deny that an

[1] Lecture republished in *Cornhill Magazine*, March 1896.

ill-written biography, if strictly true and furnished with sufficient detail, can both interest and delight. But the pleasure thereby conveyed is something different from the response which should be aroused by "pure" biography; it is merely the pleasure of satisfied curiosity analogous to that purveyed by diaries, journals, or confessions. The "pure" biography should stimulate a far deeper response. Curiosity will, of course, be both awakened and allayed; but this is incidental; the essential response will be something more than curiosity, something more complex even than acute psychological interest: sympathy and pity will be stimulated, intricate associations will be evoked—those "parallel circumstances and kindred images" to which, as Dr. Johnson saw, "we readily conform our minds." There must be result for the reader, an active and not merely a passive adjustment of sympathy; there must result for him an acquisition not of facts only but of experience; there must remain for him a definite mental impression, an altered attitude of mind. There must finally be a consciousness of creation, a conviction that some creative mind has selected and composed these facts in such a manner as to give to them a convincing interpretation; that, in a word, the given biography is a work of intelligence.

I do not think that it is necessary at this stage to say anything further regarding "pure" and "impure" biography. I have defined the former as the truthful and deliberate record of an individual's life written as a work of intelligence; I have indicated that biography becomes "impure" when it is either untruthful or unintelligent, or concerned with considerations extraneous to its own purposes. It remains for me to differentiate biography from the cognate arts of self-portraiture, memoirs, diaries, and confessions. It must be admitted that these engaging branches of literature furnish a response closely analogous to that provoked by all but the very purest biographies. They stimulate curiosity; they awaken intense psychological interest. In many cases (as in the letters of Walpole, Byron, and Mrs. Carlyle; as in the confessions of Rousseau, Goethe, Novalis, Amiel, and Haydon; as in the memoirs of Trelawny and Hickey or in the diaries of Pepys and Evelyn) the interest aroused is even greater than that which could be evoked by the most perfect biography. We are not discussing, however, the degree of interest which may or may not be stimulated by various branches of literature; we are examining the history of the art of British biography; and although, as will be seen, the arts of the diarist and

[sidenote: Relation of "pure" biography to memoirs, journals, and autobiographies.]

letter-writer have an important bearing upon biography, yet they remain distinct, they do not fall within the definition of biography as such. Autobiography occupies an intermediate position between pure biography on the one hand and mere self-portraiture on the other. A work such as Gibbon's autobiography is clearly a deliberate record of an individual's life written as a work of art. But is it essentially truthful, has any autobiographer yet attained to the detachment necessary to convey truth convincingly? Gibbon's autobiography is perhaps the best of its kind in England. And yet does it convey any complete picture of that stout and sexless historian? A gentle philosophic student with a dash of vanity—and yet we know full well that the real Gibbon was both more and less than that. I do not exclude autobiography completely; I merely state the fact that I have not, as yet, read an autobiography by which I was absolutely convinced. It is possible, if one is both intelligent and detached, to diagnose one's own temperament. But creative biography necessitates something more than diagnosis: it necessitates a scientific autopsy; and this sense of a rigorous post-mortem is just what the autobiographist has always found it impossible to convey. I foresee a great future for English autobiography, but I do not pretend that it has had a great past. I agree with Cowley. "It is," he writes, "a hard and nice subject for a man to write of himself; it grates his own heart to say anything of disparagement, and the reader's ears to hear anything of praise from him."

Having thus differentiated what I consider to be the essentials of pure biography, I propose to trace these essentials as variously manifested in the history of biography in England. It is a story of arrested development. For even today English biography is still in its infancy: it was scarcely thought of, it had not even a name, before 1683; its legitimacy was hardly recognised before 1791; it possesses a most unfortunate heredity; it suffers from many congenital defects; and its collaterals behave with such frequent vulgarity as to bring it into disrepute. And yet English biography, in spite of its shabby relations and its mixed ancestry, is in fact a perfectly respectable branch of literature. All that is necessary is to accord it a name and a dignity of its own. Its unfortunate history, which I shall now proceed to recount, will, I trust, convince you that bad biography is by no means good biography's fault.

Consider its origins. The only certain factor in

life is death; and even the behaviourists might allow to human nature the instinct of self-preservation, the instinct to defy annihilation. It is to this instinct that biography, unfortunately, owes its origin: even today the commemorative instinct, the cenotaph-urge, falsifies the art of biography, replacing the clinical arc-lamp by the muffled candles of the mortuary. Myth, legend, epic, elegy have prospered on this very soil; but biography, being I fear of ranker growth, has merely run to leaf. We can trace the ancestry of English biography to the ancient runic inscriptions which celebrated the lives of heroes and recorded the exploits of deceased and legendary warriors. We can trace it again to the old sagas and epics, to such strange parentage as Beowulf or the Widsith fragment. It is descended, maybe in the female line, from the earlier elegies, from Deor, from *The Wanderer*, from *The Wife's Complaint*.

Origins of biography. (1) The commemorative instinct.

With the sixth century the commemorative strain in English biography mingles with a didactic strain —an equally pregnant source of bad biography. The lives of the eminent are used and abused for the purposes of ethical teaching or theological argument. Hagiography begins. The turgid denunciations of Gildas

(2) The didactic temptation. Hagiography.

the Wise (*flor.* 547) mark a break with the runic tradition, and in the *Historia Brittonum* over a century later the long succession of hagiographies is introduced by a life of St. Patrick. Adamnan's *Life of St. Columba* was written about 690, and thereafter we have Aldhelm (d. 709) with his lives of several distinguished virgins, and Eddius Stephanus with his life of Wilfrid. With the advent of Bede (d. 735) we enter for the first time upon the dawn of literary narrative in England. Bede was the first among these muddled hagiographers to manifest a sense of literary construction; he improved upon the turgid tradition of previous monastic writers and wrote with a personal note of simplicity and tenderness. His *Martyrology* was immensely popular; his metrical life of St. Cuthbert was less successful than his prose study of that dignitary; but his importance to us lies in his real gift of selection—in the vividness, for instance, with which, in the second book of his *Ecclesiastical History*, he has introduced the image of the sparrow fluttering through the light and smoke of the hall and out again into the night beyond. Bede, for all this, remains a hagiographer: he insists that it is necessary to say "good things of good men" and "evil things of wicked persons"; his ethical didacticism is only too apparent; and although at moments one can detect a note of scepticism, a note even of scholarly inquiry, yet Bede in general accepts the miraculous and the legendary with the usual monastic gullibility. The several lives of saints which preceded and succeeded Bede—such works as the anonymous biographies of St. Cuthbert, the *Life of Guthlac* by Felix, and the *Life of St. Willibrord* by Alcuin—need scarcely detain us. It is necessary only to note that hagiographies and martyrologies blossomed innumerable, and that they created a persistent tradition extending well into the thirteenth century and beyond. It was a bad tradition. The centre of interest was never the individual but always the institution; their insistence on the ethical message allowed the hagiographers no scope for insight or even accuracy; the desire to prove their case induced them to insert the legendary, the supernatural, and the miraculous. These prose and verse lives were the novels of the Middle Ages, but their influence upon biography was regrettable.

In the ninth century was written the first biography of an English layman, the *Life of Alfred the Great*, by Bishop Asser. The authenticity of this work has been disputed, but it represents an endeavour on the part of a certain individual, whether Bishop Asser or another, to compose a definite portrait of an arresting

Asser's "Life of Alfred."

personality with whom he had for many years been intimate. It is not a very successful endeavour. Our curiosity and our expectation are early aroused by the author's announcement of his purpose. He proposes, he says, to write down "aliquantulum, quantum notitiæ meæ innotuerit, de vita et moribus et æqua conversatione atque, ex parte non modica, res gestas domini mei Ælfredi."[1] This is promising; what follows, however, is an ornate jumble of chronicle and notes written in the most monastic Latin and conveying but a slight impression of King Alfred's character, development, or personality. There emerges, of course, the conventional picture of the devout, industrious, chaste, and scholarly king, but the "æqua conversatio" gives us little more than a few unconvincing compliments indicative of the high esteem with which Asser was himself regarded by his master, and even the story of the cakes and the cowherd's wife is, it is to be feared, a later interpolation. I am not convinced by Asser's *Alfred*: the genealogy, for instance, goes back to Adam; there is much irrelevant discourse; there are few lights and shadows, and some very unsatisfactory explanations, as when Asser excuses his long absence from both the Court and his own diocese by stating that he caught fever at Winchester and took

[1] Asser, Clarendon Press edition, c. 74.

to his bed for thirteen months. I do not believe that explanation, and it is the introduction of similar evasive improbabilities that throws a veil of unreality over the whole biography. Once only, and in a little matter, does Asser really satisfy the curiosity which his introduction arouses. It is in connection with King Alfred's candles: "Sed cum aliquando . . . candelæ ardendo lucescere non poterant, nimirum ventorum violentia inflante, quæ aliquando per ecclesiarum ostia et fenestrarum, maceriarum quoque atque tabularum, vel frequentes parietum rimulas, nec non et tentoriorum tenuitates, die noctuque sine intermissione flabat, . . . excogitavit unde talem ventorum sufflationem prohibere potuisset, consilioque artificiose atque sapienter invento, laternam ex lignis et bovinis cornibus pulcherrime construere imperavit. . . ."[1] This passage, while giving the full relish of Asser's absurd style, has the convincing merit of a thing directly observed.

On leaving Asser we plunge into the period of the English chronicle. Biography proper disappears in the writing of annals; and although hagiography continues, as in Wulfstan's homilies, and improves, as in Ælfric's *Lives of the Saints*, yet it remains hagiography, and the old

The chronicles.

[1] Asser, Clarendon Press edition, c. 104.

gossip about portents, miracles, and curses, the old involved traditions of monastic Latin, go on and on. This uniform mediocrity is not relieved till we reach the early twelfth century, and the *Historia Novorum* and *Vita Anselmi*

Eadmer. by Eadmer the monk of Canterbury. Eadmer deserves very honourable mention in any history of our national biography; his merit was recognised by his successors. "Eadmer," writes William of Malmesbury, "has told everything so lucidly that he seems somehow to have placed events before our very eyes. He has so arranged the letters as to support and verify his assertions in the most decisive way." This is a telling tribute to the real biographical method, and Eadmer fully merits such praise. His Latin is simple and direct; something of the tender fierceness of Anselm inspires his whole attitude; the introduction of letters anticipates the method of Mason and Boswell; and his records of conversation, his records of dramatic incidents, are written with a vividness and a power of selection which render the work unquestionably the first "pure" biography written in this country.

With the twelfth century comes one of the most
William of potent factors in the development of
Malmesbury. biography, namely, the birth of curiosity. It was a premature birth, and curiosity, until

the seventeenth century, showed signs of arrested development. Men like William of Malmesbury, however, rendered immense service in freeing history, and through history biography, from the brambles of monasticism and the thickets of the older chronicles. William of Malmesbury possessed a conscious literary purpose: he believed in history as an art of creation; he controlled his material and moulded it into a definite shape; he possessed imagination, style, and humour; above all, he was immensely inquisitive. "A variety of anecdote," he writes, "cannot be displeasing to any one, unless he be morose enough to rival the superciliousness of Cato." He loved vivid detail; he delighted in images and associations. Take this, for instance, from his description of the enthusiasm aroused by the first Crusade: "The Welshman left his hunting, the Scot his fellowship with vermin, the Dane his drinking-party, the Norwegian his raw fish. Lands were deserted of their husbandmen; houses of their inhabitants: even whole cities migrated. There was no regard to relationship; affection to their country was held in little esteem . . . they hungered and thirsted after Jerusalem alone. . . ." This is indeed an advance upon the arid credulity, the illiterate annals, of the early chroniclers. The stimulus of curiosity, the realisation that past events and characters are of intrinsic interest in themselves, are again noticeable in the work of Geoffrey of Monmouth, who flung over his history the colours of Arthurian romance. Geoffrey indeed was a precursor of Ossian, and even as Macpherson he referred cryptically to "the book in the British speech which Walter brought out from Brittany." Such romanticism was all to the good, and affected not adversely the ensuing century, the golden age of the monastic historian. Prominent among the thirteenth-century chroniclers was Matthew Paris, historiographer of St. Albans, who in compiling his chronicle adopted a seriously critical attitude, and endeavoured honestly to reach the truth. Mention must also be made of Adam of Eynsham's "great life" of Hugh, Bishop of Lincoln (1212-20). This work, inevitably, is a panegyric; but it repudiates the miraculous, and it displays the germs of accuracy and direct observation. Hagiography was dying down. The first stage of English history was also drawing to its close. The fourteenth century coincided with a decline in patriotism; the educated world bathed in the gentle rays of romance and internationalism; the charm of fiction checked the growing interest in fact. The chronicles, the homilies, the lives of saints became

ORIGINS OF ENGLISH BIOGRAPHY

shorter and more perfunctory; the wind which had filled the sails of Eadmer and William of Malmesbury ceased to blow. The Court thought only of the French romances; the monasteries deteriorated into scholasticism; and public opinion was interested mainly in immediate material concerns. We are accustomed thus to define the fourteenth century, to represent it as a languid and fanciful period in which all educated interest in facts suffered an eclipse. And yet there is Chaucer, the greatest of English realists, a man who possessed all the energies and all the faculties of the supreme biographer: curiosity, acute psychological observation, humour, sympathy, immense synthetic force, a genius for selection—such were the gifts which Chaucer, had he wished, could have brought to biography. What lives could Chaucer have written of his acquaintance Petrarch or his patron John of Gaunt—inaccurate perhaps, obscene possibly, but overwhelmingly vivid and convincing! But Chaucer wrote no biographies, for his contemporaries were not interested in that particular form of literary creation. They were interested, not in the real but in the unreal, not in England but in France and Italy. That Chaucer, in his third period, should have been able to cast the slough of French and Italian models and exploit the more robust vein of English tradi-

Chaucer.

tion, indicates that the influence of the Continent was superficial rather than profound. But however superficial, it sufficed to stem the interest in national history throughout the fourteenth century. The century that follows is an intellectual blank. While the Continent was stirring with the sap of humanism, England traversed the most shrouded phase of her intelligence. The Paston letters are sufficient to show us how completely all intellectual curiosity had decayed: the fifteenth century is the most depressing period in the whole history of British genius. In biography it has only one important document to show—John Boston's catalogue of the Abbey libraries, with notes on the authors. This work, which was never printed, was read in manuscript by later antiquarians, and is largely responsible for the inaccuracies in which they abound.

It is not, therefore, until the sixteenth century that, with the renewal of patriotism and with the dissolution of the religious houses, the old energetic interest in history revived. The Tudor chronicles share to the full the faults of their predecessors: there is the same uncontrollable irrelevancy, the same incessant preoccupation with comets, and strange portents and monstrous births. But there is a fresh feeling about it all, a

The sixteenth century.

gay inquisitiveness, a real desire to know, to find out, and to write it all down. There is Hall's chronicle, in parts "clouted up together" from second-hand material, but in parts showing real observation, a real liking for urban events, for London, for Henry VIII, for people walking about streets, for processions and for masquerades. There is the collection made by Holinshed (1578), and particularly that portion of it which contains William Harrison's *Description of England*. There are John Stow and John Speed. There are the twenty-seven Latin volumes of Polydore Vergil of Urbino. There are Camden's *Annals*. There is the unfortunate John Leland, who toured England making copious and disjointed notes of everything he saw and everybody he heard of. These notes accumulated; they accumulated to his own despair. It was impossible to get them into any sort of order. John Leland became completely inarticulate. "Except," he protested, "truth be delycately clothed in purpure her written veryties can scarce fynde a reader." And so Leland relapsed into insanity, and his "written veryties" were purloined by the Bishop of Ossory and Mr. Pits. In 1563 came Foxe's *Acts and Monuments*, that blood-soaked martyrology which enjoyed universal popularity, and which with its vivid zest for tortures at least pandered to the growing taste for realism. And in 1579 was published North's translation of *Plutarch*—a book which, as I shall show, exercised an immense and fatal influence on English biography in the century that followed.

Before, however, I leave the sixteenth century it is necessary to examine in some detail the few bio-
<small>Minor biographies of the sixteenth century.</small> graphies that were actually composed between 1530 and 1600. There is the *History of Richard III*, which has been ascribed to Thomas More, but was more probably composed by Cardinal Morton. This book is written in good English, with a vivid sense of the picturesque and a very heightened sense of drama. But the author's attitude is not scientific, and the portrait of the central character is too uniformly dark to carry conviction. The works of Sir John Hayward (*First Part of the Raigne of King Henrie IV* (1599) and his subsequent books on the Norman Kings and Edward VI) deserve mention as being definite attempts to cast narrative into a literary form. They are represented as being serious, scholarly, and dull. They teem, it appears, with adaptations from Tacitus. I have not read these works.

There were two biographies, however, written in

the sixteenth century which are of considerable interest and importance. The first is Roper's *More;* the second, Cavendish's *Wolsey.* William Roper (1496-1578) married Margaret, the favourite daughter of Thomas More, and lived for many years as a bewildered member of the family in Chelsea. His biography of his father-in-law appears to have been written shortly after the latter's execution in 1535, although it was not published till 1626, and then only in Paris. The book is generally (and somewhat misleadingly) referred to as the first English biography. It would be more accurate to describe it as the first sustained narrative of an individual's life written in the English language. Roper, as a biographer, has his faults. He was an ardent Catholic, and wrote with bias; he was not very intelligent, and had little interest in what he could not understand: there was a great deal, moreover, which Roper could not understand. We learn nothing from his book of Erasmus, or Holbein, or the *Utopia,* or even the real causes of More's dismissal. He was not a very skilled manipulator of material, and his book is ultimately a series of vivid reminiscences of varying importance. Moreover, he was inaccurate. He undermines one's belief by stating that More was executed in 1537. His devotion to his father-in-

Roper's "Life of Sir Thomas More."

law, the cenotaph-atmosphere which pervades his biography, leads him to slur over many topics which it would have been interesting, and more honest, to discuss. He represents More as having been far more courageous and independent when Speaker of the House of Commons than was actually the case. He leaves us wondering how More, if really so stainless, was able to reconcile his conscience with the function of Chancellor to Henry VIII. He gives us no indication that his hero, in spite of many splendid passages in *Utopia*, was intolerant in religious matters and often cruel. Foxe refers to More as "a bitter persecutor of good men"; Hall speaks of him as "a great persecutor of such as detested the supremacy of the Bishop of Rome"; and to Froude he is simply "a merciless bigot." Such authorities are not very reliable, but one would wish none the less that Roper had dealt with the accusation, or had at least provided some material with which it might be countered. For reasons such as these Roper's *Life* can scarcely be hailed as a "pure" biography; it is too commemorative, too incomplete, too biassed, and too ill-constructed. But it is eminently readable and eminently vivid. It is in fact his genius for direct and varied narrative and dialogue which gives Roper so important a place in the history of British biography. Take this, for

ORIGINS OF ENGLISH BIOGRAPHY

instance, as a representation of the intimate relations existing between the King and his Chancellor:

> And otherwise would he in the night have him up into the leades, there to consider with him the diversities, courses, motions and operations of the Stars and Planetts. ... And for the pleasure he took in his companie would his Grace sodenly somtymes come home to his house at Chelsie to be merry with him, withere on a tyme unlooked for he came to dinner, and after dinner in a faire garden of his walked with him by the space of an houre houlding his arms about his neck.[1]

His handling of dialogue also is far in advance of anything that had existed since Eadmer. There is the tragic farewell between Megge More and her father, and there is that curious intrusion of his mother-in-law as a comic relief. The passage is worth quoting. Lady More visits her husband in the Tower, "comminge like a simple woman and somewhat worldlie too," and urges him to apologise to the King, to make his peace and to return to his house and garden in Chelsea. The following dialogue ensues:—

> "I praye thee good Mistress Alice tell me, tell me one thynge."
> "What is that?" quoth she.
> "Is not this house as nighe heaven as myne owne?"
> To whom she, after her accustomed fashion, not likeinge such talke, answered, "Tille valle, Tille valle."

[1] Roper's *More*, Pitt Press Series (1897), pp. ix, 1, 23, 26; pp. xiv, 1, 31-36.

"How say you, Mistress Alice, is it not soe?" quoth he.
"Bone Deus, bone Deus, man, will this geere never be left?" quoth she.
So her persuasions moved him but a little.[1]

Here we have good psychology, excellently rendered. Whatever faults of construction and omission may sully Roper's book, such writing goes far to redeem them, and to give the book a recognisable artistic quality.

To George Cavendish (1500-61) has been ascribed "the glory of having given to English litera-
Cavendish's "Wolsey." ture the first specimen of artistic biography."[2] This, although somewhat unfair on William Roper, is substantially true. The *Life of Wolsey* is a far more self-conscious and deliberate production than the *Life of More*. It is a work of art and not an accident. In the first place, it was written between July 1554 and February 1557; that is more than twenty-four years after the events recorded, and it acquires from this circumstance an impressive atmosphere of detachment, a very convincing perspective. In the second place, it was composed as a definite theme or thesis to illustrate the mutability of human fortunes. And in the third place, it is written with real literary talent,

[1] Roper's *More*, Pitt Press Series (1897), pp. xiv, 1, 6-35.
[2] *Cambridge History of English Literature*, vol. iii, p. 336.

with admirable lucidity, tenderness, and charm. The real triumph of Cavendish lies in the skill with which, while profiting by the unity given to his work by a didactic purpose—or, as I should prefer to say, by his thesis—he is yet able to keep that purpose consistently in the background, and to write what is essentially an "impure," because a didactic, biography, in the manner and with the success of one of the "purest" biographies ever composed. The thesis of mutability is implicit, but not explicit, throughout the volume; it is only in the concluding paragraphs that the lesson is drawn, and that in a burst of wholly apposite rhetoric:

> Who list to read and consider with an indifferent eye this history, may behold the wondrous mutability of vain honours, the brittle assurance of abundance, the uncertainty of dignities, the flattering of feigned friends, and the fickle trust of worldly powers. . . . O madness! O foolish desire! O fond hope! O greedy desire of vain honours, dignities and riches! O what inconstant trust and assurance is in rolling fortune! [1]

Curiosity is deliberately aroused and stimulated. "Fortune smiled so upon him," writes Cavendish in one of his early pages, "but to what end she brought

[1] *Life of Cardinal Wolsey*, by Geo. Cavendish, edited by Samuel Singer, 2nd edition, 1827, p. 405.

him, ye shall hear after."[1] He knows, also, how to dissociate himself from his hero, so as to create at the outset the necessary impression of detached observation. "In whom," he writes of the young Wolsey, "the King conceived such a loving fantasy and in especial for that he was most earnest and readiest among all the council to advance the King's only will and pleasure, without any respect to the case." "So far," he writes again, "as the other counsellors advised the King to leave his pleasures and to attend to the affairs of the realm, so busily did the almoner (Wolsey) persuade him to the contrary which delighted him much and caused him to have the greater affection to the almoner."[2] Against such a background of apparent disloyalty to Wolsey, the real affection and admiration which he felt for the Cardinal is conveyed with heightened effect. We start by regarding Cavendish as anything but an apologist for Wolsey, and his ultimate defence finds us in a mood of confidence ready to be convinced. It is very skilful of Cavendish to create such an impression, and it is deliberately done. The actual narrative, also, is treated with conscious artistic intention. Cavendish is always present, but

[1] *Life of Cardinal Wolsey*, by Geo. Cavendish, edited by Samuel Singer, 2nd edition, 1827, p. 82.
[2] *Ibid.*, p. 81.

always discreetly in the background, or waiting even "in the adjoining chamber." His visual memory is remarkable. He tells of Wolsey smelling at his vinegar-orange when pestered by suitors, of Lord Wiltshire's sobbing beside his bedside, of the Cardinal's flinging himself boyishly off his mule at Putney Bridge, of Queen Katharine's broken English, of Dr. Augustine "with his boisterous gown of black velvet upon him" upsetting Wolsey's great silver cross which had been propped against the tapestry, of the Earl of Northumberland's embarrassment at Cawood Castle: "these two lords standing at a window by the chimney, in my lord's bedchamber, the Earl trembling said with a very faint and soft voice, unto my lord (laying his hand upon his arm), 'My lord, I arrest you of high treason.'" And from then on the tragedy hastens through the squalid details of Wolsey's illness to his death and burial. The final scene is laid at Hampton Court, where Cavendish had repaired after his master's death. The King behaved well to him, and the book is enabled thereby to end on a pleasing note of poetic justice. The whole incident is recorded in Cavendish's most skilful manner:

> Upon the morrow I was sent for by the King to come to his Grace: and repairing to the King I found him shooting at the rounds in the park, on the backside of

the garden. And perceiving him occupied in shooting, thought it not my duty to trouble him: but leaned to a tree, intending to stand there and to attend his gracious pleasure. Being in a great study, at the last the King came suddenly behind me where I stood and clapped his hand upon my shoulder: and when I perceived him, I fell upon my knee.

In which pleasant posture I shall leave this earliest master of the art of English biography.

We must be careful not to exaggerate the influence and importance of Roper and Cavendish.

Biography as it stood in 1599.
We must bear in mind that their works were available to their contemporaries and immediate successors in manuscript only and not in print. But none the less both Cavendish and Roper mark an immense advance. They are imbued doubtless with the old commemorative instinct; their books are marred by no small proportion of didacticism; they have not broken finally (we ourselves have not broken finally) with the old runic inscription, with the long tradition of hagiography. But the centre of interest, the *emphasis* of their curiosity, has shifted: they neither of them regard their subjects as types representative of institutions, but as individuals representative of human personality; they are more interested in the internal than the external, in character than in action. It is owing to them that English biography

ORIGINS OF ENGLISH BIOGRAPHY

was first differentiated as a species of literary composition distinct from history and romance. There can be little doubt that had English biography developed undisturbed from the strain of Roper and Cavendish it would have reached its full flowering a century before 1791. Unfortunately, however, the seventeenth century, for all its vivid realism and curiosity, grafted upon our healthy native stock a further element extraneous to pure biography. In my next lecture I shall trace the influence, the disastrous influence, of Plutarch, of Theophrastus, and the French school of character-sketches. For the seventeenth century to the student of English biography is a great disappointment.

II

THE SEVENTEENTH CENTURY, 1599-1667

Nature of seventeenth-century biography—The character-sketch—Seventeenth-century history—Bacon's *Henry VII*—Clarendon—The realistic tradition—Aubrey—Anthony à Wood—Fuller's *Worthies*—Seventeenth-century *ana*—Seventeenth-century memoirs—Lord Herbert of Cherbury—Lady Fanshawe—Mrs. Hutchinson—Duchess of Newcastle.

THE seventeenth century, as I have indicated, offered an immense opportunity. The opportunity was missed. All the essential elements of biography were either existent or discovered between 1600 and 1700: there was widespread public curiosity, acute psychological interest, accurate scholarship, immense capacity for industry, a real desire to produce creative and artistic history, and, as a vehicle, the perfection of English prose. The seventeenth century in England can boast, it is true, of Walton's *Lives*; but its most typical products were the funeral orations of Jeremy Taylor and the equally commemorative oration of Dr. Sprat. There are several accidents which account for this miscar-

THE SEVENTEENTH CENTURY

riage. In the first place, the political condition of the country was too disturbed, and the moral conflict too intense, for writers to have either the leisure, the courage, or the detachment necessary for pure biography. In the second place, the potential biographers of the century tended either to accumulate scraps of information, or to write journals, or, as Clarendon and Bacon, to create an art of English history. And in the third place, the influence of Plutarch and of the Theophrastians inclined people to be interested rather in typical "characters" than in individual temperaments; to write on the deductive rather than the inductive method, and thereby to cast their biographies in an artificial and unconvincing mould. It is with the origin and growth of the "character-sketch" that I first propose to deal.

I have already said that North's very vivid and individual rendering of Amyot's *Plutarch* was first published in 1579. It achieved immediate popularity and ran into five editions between 1579 and 1631. Similar translations followed. Holland produced his Livy in 1600 and his Suetonius in 1606; Grenewey's translations of Tacitus had already begun to appear in 1598, and were issued successively in the five years that followed; Sir H. Savile's rendering of the *Annals*

The character-sketch.

and the *Agricola* ran through six editions between 1591 and 1640; Hobbe's Thucydides dates from 1629 and Heywood's Sallust from 1633. The influence of Tacitus was predominant throughout the century, and was supplemented by contemporary continental imitators. The English exiles in France, moreover, caught the infection of the French memoir and introduced it into England. Everybody began to write memoirs and journals, but they thought it safer not to publish them. More specific was the influence of such "romances" as Madame de Scudéry's *Artamene, or Le Grand Cyrus*, in which contemporary portraits were introduced under transparent pseudonyms. The popularity of these romances led the intellectuals of Mlle. de Montpensier's circle to discard the pseudonyms and to write portraits of each other. The influence of these essays in psychological analysis is very apparent in the work of Clarendon. It is possible, however, to exaggerate their general influence in England. *Le Grand Cyrus*, it is true, was the only begetter of Mrs. Manley's *New Atalantis;* but the latter work was not published till 1709 and its success was only momentary. Character-sketches occurred, but they were not directly imitated from French models. Rather were they drawn from Tacitus, or, more specifically, from Theophrastus,

THE SEVENTEENTH CENTURY

the heir and successor of Aristotle, whose *ethical characters* were translated into Latin by Casaubon in 1592. This book became immediately popular and ran into six editions within a few years. As many as fifty-six imitations of Theophrastus were published between 1605 and 1700, the more notable being Hall's *Characteristics of Virtues and Vices* (1608), Sir Thomas Overbury's *Characters or Witty Descriptions of the Properties of Sundry Persons* (1614), and Bishop Earle's *Microcosmographie* (1608). The popularity of the Theophrastian character-sketch gave method and unity to psychological investigation. But its influence was in other ways harmful: it led biographers to fix upon a certain quality or type, and subsequently so to adjust the details as to fit them into the thesis or frame selected. This deductive method, which is opposed to the inductive realism of our native genius, can be recognised in many of the historical portraits of the period, and it is this which prevents Walton's *Lives* from attaining to the perfection of pure biography.

It is indeed unfortunate that these external influences should have marred English biography in the seventeenth century, since in the cognate branches of history and personal reminiscences immense progress was made. The influence which this progress exer-

Seventeenth-century history.

cised on biography itself was important, and some examination must therefore be made, firstly, of seventeenth-century history, and secondly, of seventeenth-century journals and memoirs. Already by the end of the previous century our intellectuals were distressed that English literature, so rich in other branches, should have produced no history worthy of the name. Sir W. Raleigh had, and from personal experience, defined one of the main causes of this deficiency. "Whosoever," he wrote in the Introduction to his *History of the World*, "in writing a moderne Historie shall follow truth too neare the heeles, it may haply strike out his teeth." In his *Advancement of Learning* Bacon drew attention to out national poverty in this branch of literature, and it was doubtless with this reproach in mind that Sir J. Hayward, in his lives of the kings, deliberately essayed to compose an artistic historical work and was thrown into the Tower for his pains. Bacon himself, however, in 1621 wrote his *Historie of the Reigne of Henry VII*, a work of considerable importance and one which merits more detailed consideration.

This book, which was written with one wary eye upon James I, purports to be a biography. Bacon asserts that he is primarily concerned with the history of a single individual.

Bacon's "Henry VII."

THE SEVENTEENTH CENTURY

"I have not flattered him," he says, "but took him to life as well as I could, sitting so far off and having no better light." This is all very well; but in fact the book is not a biography at all, but a history of events from 1485 to 1509, in which, as was inevitable, Henry VII is the central figure. There is no attempt to produce any detached or vivid picture of this central figure, or to deal with his life prior to Bosworth field. The King's character—his caution, his rapacity, his stinginess, his reserve, his "manner of showing things by pieces and by dark lights"— emerges from the story in but a shadowy and unconvincing shape. There are long digressions on the legislation of the period, and several inaccuracies which are well indicated in Dr. Lumley's Introduction to the Pitt Press edition. The style is marred by lapses into the old manner of the chronicles, and frequent are the paragraphs which begin "This yeare . . ." One has the impression that Bacon, if interested at all, was interested only in drawing apposite parallels. There is little direct research or personal interpretation. Bacon admits that his authorities were "naked and negligent"; but he follows them none the less, and his book is a disappointment. It does not deal with an individual, it is not very truthful, and it is not a work of art.

With Clarendon we approach far closer to history, and incidentally to biography, composed as creative literature. Clarendon had learnt much from the classics, and even more from his long residence in France. He was the first Englishman to regard history, if not scientifically, if not even philosophically, then at least from the literary point of view. His position as our first great historian is so thoroughly established that it is unnecessary for me to do more than indicate the extent to which he influenced and developed the cognate art of biography. For Clarendon was the first to lay down the principle that history deals not only with facts but with human beings, that the problems of history are concerned primarily with human personality. For him the historian should do more than chronicle events; he should introduce "a lively representation of persons," and his own history therefore is in fact a gallery of portraits. That these portraits are not better done is due to a variety of causes. In the first place, Clarendon's *History* is a fusion of two separate books and lacks unity of impression. In the second place, Clarendon, who was steeped in the French manner, in Tacitus, and in the Theophrastians, was interested rather in ethical types than in individual psychology. His characters are admirably composed,

[margin: Clarendon's "History of the Rebellion."]

but they lack distinctive relief; his dramatic sense is stronger than his sense of the pictorial; he is synthetic rather than analytical; he has little concern with personal idiosyncrasies. Clarendon's method is thus to personify qualities. He succeeds admirably, but his very success popularised the Theophrastian method of treating historical characters as ethical types, and the method persisted, through Burnet and Halifax, to Macaulay and Carlyle.

It is essential to bear in mind that the character-sketch (by which I mean not only the specialised French and Theophrastian forms, but the wider tradition deriving from Tacitus, Suetonius, and Plutarch) became in the seventeenth century a recognised and habitual form of historical or elegant portraiture. It was the prose analogue of metaphysical poetry. This unfortunate circumstance explains why the more robust and realistic tradition, inherent in our native genius (a tradition which I should wish to call "the Chaucer tradition"), although it also showed a remarkable development in the same century, failed for the moment to produce any noticeable effect. This tradition was manifested predominantly in the work of Aubrey, a man who, had he been granted the gift of sustained industry, might well have been our greatest biographical genius. It was manifested,

The realistic tradition.

secondarily, in the great mass of memoir-literature which the seventeenth century produced. I shall deal first with Aubrey and his colleagues.

John Aubrey (1626-98) became interested in biography almost by chance and in order to oblige a friend. This friend was Anthony Wood (or Anthony à Wood as he so romantically styled himself), who towards the end of the century embarked upon a sort of biographical dictionary which was in 1691 published under the name of *Athenæ Oxonienses*. In 1667 Wood had met Aubrey and had asked him to assist in collecting anecdotes and information. Aubrey was at the moment at a loose end. The year 1666 had not been very satisfactory: "This yeare," he writes, "all my businesses and affaires ran kim kam." Wood's suggestion was a helpful suggestion—at least it offered a diversion; at least it was something to do. Aubrey was a little tired by then of being an antiquarian. It had been very exciting discovering the megalithic remains at Avebury; but the oddities of one's contemporaries were even more enthralling and far less trouble. So Aubrey embarked upon his "Minutes." They grew and grew, and as they grew his taste for what had started merely as an additional hobby became overpowering. In 1680 we find him writing to Wood: "It will be a pretty thing

Aubrey.

and I am glad you put me on it. I doe it playingly."[1] Or again (15th June 1680): "I have, according to your desire, putt in writing these minutes of lives tumultuarily as they occurred to my thoughts or as occasionally I had information of them."[2] It is this playful and tumultuous method which renders Aubrey's *Minutes of Lives* little more than a brilliant card-index. For Aubrey, as Wood himself wrote, was "a shiftless person, roving and magotie-headed." And his work suffered accordingly. In Mr. Andrew Clark's edition you can read this index in a convenient form and with much profit and entertainment. For Aubrey had all the talents of a born biographer, excepting only industry and method. His desire for truth, marred only by his prejudice against the Herbert family, is highly commendable. In his letter to Wood above quoted he describes his notes as containing "the naked and plaine truth, which is here exposed so bare that the very pudenda are not covered. . . . So that after your perusall I must desire you to make a castration . . . and sow on some figge-leaves." On which hint Wood, who was a pedant, destroyed some forty-four pages. But the Ashmolean

---

[1] MS., Bonard, 14, fol. 131.
[2] MS., Aubrey, 6, fol. 12. Quoted in Andrew Clark's edition, p. 10.

manuscript remains. It furnishes ample proof of Aubrey's astounding gifts of observation, insight, and humour. Take this as an entry for John Birkenhead: "He was exceedingly confident (κυνώπης), witty, not very grateful to his benefactors, would lye damnably. He was of midaling stature, great goggli eies. Not of a sweet aspect. . . ."[1] Take this again from the notes on Francis Bacon: "He had a delicate lively hazel eie and Dr. Harvey told me it was like the eie of a viper. I have now forgott what Mr. Bushell sayd, whether his lordship enjoyed his Muse best at night or in the morning." It is to be feared that Aubrey frequently forgot what Mr. Bushell said. In one instance in particular his dilatoriness has robbed us of the most tantalising information. I quote from the card-index on Mr. William Beeston, which is very typical of Aubrey's method.

William Beeston. (16 -1682)
Did I tell you that I have met with old Mr. ——— [2] who knew all the old English poets, whose lives I am taking from him. His father was master of the ——— playhouse.

W. Shakespeare Quære. Mr. Beeston who knowes most of him from Mr. Lacey. He lives in Shoreditch at Hog Lane within 6 dores of Folgate. Quære etiam for Ben Jonson. Old Mr. Beeston whom Mr. Dreyden calls "the chronicle of the stage" died at his home in Bishops-

[1] Andrew Clark's edition, p. 105.
[2] The blanks are Aubrey's own.

gate Street Without, about Bartholomews tyde 1682. Mr. Shipley in Somerset House hath his papers.[1]

It is evident that this Beeston *dossier* consisted of three separate notes written probably at intervals of several years. In the first note Aubrey records that he has met Mr. Beeston, and it was probably on that occasion that he obtained from him the story of Shakespeare having been a village schoolmaster. The second note is a cross-reference from Shakespeare's *dossier* reminding Aubrey to call again on Beeston and obtain further information. The third note records Beeston's death. If only Aubrey had followed up his intention of thoroughly pumping Mr. Beeston he would certainly have left us details far more copious than those which actually figure on the card-index for Ben Jonson and Shakespeare. For, in general, Aubrey had a passion for vivid detail, whether it be Edmund Waller's "full eie popping out and working," or the way Milton pronounced the letter "r," or Hobbes's habit of keeping pen and ink in his walking-stick and scribbling "so soon as a thought darted," or the following intimate picture of the author of *Leviathan:*—

> He had always bookes of prick-song lyeing on his table . . . which at night, when he was abed and the doors made fast and was sure nobody heard him, he sang

[1] Andrew Clark's edition, vol. i, pp. 96-97.

aloud (not that he had a very good voice) but for his health's sake: he did believe it did his lungs good and conduced much to prolong his life.[1]

I turn with regret from the exhilarating Aubrey to his employer, Anthony à Wood (1632-95), a highly disagreeable pedant who sought to justify his real malignity on the ground that "faults ought no more to be concealed than virtues, and, whatever it may be in a painter, it is no excellence in a historian to throw a veil on deformities. . . ." This opinion is admirable, but the fact remains that "the morose Wood" (I quote from Dr. Johnson) was a misanthrope, and that misanthropes should never write biography, still less biographical notes upon their contemporaries. He was himself, I am glad to say, prosecuted for libel, and his *Athenæ Oxonienses* was publicly burnt. It remains as a useful book of reference for scholars, it set the fashion for biographical collections, and it can, to that extent, claim the high honour of being (via Tanner, Jacob, Shiels, and Berkenhout) the ancestor of the *Dictionary of National Biography*.

<small>Anthony à Wood.</small>

A third such compiler of biographical notes was Thomas Fuller (1608-61), a man who has obtained undue celebrity owing to Coleridge's benediction. For Fuller is the most in-

<small>Thomas Fuller.</small>

[1] Andrew Clark's edition, vol. i, p. 352.

sufferable of all bores, the unctuous type, the self-deprecatory, the jocose. This tiresome old man compiled his *Abel Redivivus,* whereafter he toured England taking notes of county histories and antiquities, their products, their monuments, their dialects, and their celebrated men since the days of Alfred. The latter are divided, under the heading of each county, into princes, martyrs, confessors, prelates, statesmen, soldiers, writers, and so on; there are long lists of mayors and sheriffs; there is much scriptural quotation; there are incessant puns and quips—what Fuller himself calls his "pleasant passages"; and the whole thing, as he says, "is interlaced (not as meat but as condiment) with many delightful stories." Fuller possessed, however, a certain merit: although he regarded chronology as a "surly little animal" and often failed to verify his dates, yet he tried to be accurate. He had an amazing memory, but he had no biographical gift whatever. He deliberately omits all the shadows, and contends that he is bound to do so "by the rules of charity." I cannot convey a better criticism of Fuller as a biographer than by quoting his note on Donne:

> *John Donne* was born in this city of wealthy parentage extracted out of Wales: one of an excellent wit, large travel and choice experience. After many vicissitudes

in his youth, his reduced age was honoured with the doctorship of divinity and deanery of St. Paul's.

Should I endeavour to deliver his exact character I (who willingly would not do any wrong) should do a fourfold injury: (1) to his worthy memory, whose merit my pen is unable to express; (2) to myself, in undertaking what I am not sufficient to perform; (3) to the reader, first in raising, then in frustrating, his expectation; (4) to my deservedly honoured master Isaac Walton, by whom his life is so learnedly written. It is enough for me to observe that he died March 31 A.D. 1631, and lieth buried in St. Paul's under an ingenious and choice monument, neither so costly as to occasion envy, nor so common as to cause contempt.

Could anything be more futile or more frivolous? I have dealt at some length with the biographical compilations of Aubrey, Wood, and Fuller, since it was through activities and interests such as theirs that the more permanent and more natural traditions of English biography were preserved and developed. Aubrey was little influenced by Tacitus, the Theophrastians, or the French. The impulse which inspired his investigations was sheer native prying. It is this unsullied stream of intelligent curiosity, rather than the literary fashions of the ancients or the French *précieuses*, which led to Johnson, and through Johnson to Boswell and all that is more important in English biography. Thus although the seventeenth

<small>The seventeenth-century "ana."</small>

century was the age of the character-sketch, and although its influence on the art of biography was to some extent harmful, yet we must not forget that it was also, and perhaps predominantly, the age of curiosity, and that without curiosity the art of biography languishes and declines. I would refer, particularly, to the mass of *ana* which were published between 1650 and 1661. We have Worcester's *Apophthegmes* (1650), the *Regales Aphorismi* of James I, the *Cottoni Posthuma* of 1651, the *Fragmenta Aulica* of 1662, and finally the famous *Table Talk of John Selden*, which was published in 1689. This pedantic collection (an edition of which has recently been issued by Quaritch for the Selden Society) was based on the *Tischreden* of Martin Luther, and was considered by Dr. Johnson to contain more wit and wisdom than any of the French *ana* could boast. I cannot follow the doctor in his admiration for *Selden's Table Talk*. It seems to me pompous, dull, and elaborate. It is not a book which I desire to read again.

The memoirs of the seventeenth century are innumerable, and every year further hitherto unpublished journals, letters, or reminiscences are brought to light. We have the diary of Lady Anne Clifford, the memoirs of Robert Carey, Earl of Monmouth, the

Seventeenth-century memoirs.

diary of Tom Manningham, the autobiography of Sir Simonds d'Ewes, the diary of Sir H. Slingsby and that of John Rous. We have the memoirs of Sir J. Reresby, the letters of Sir H. Bulstrode, the diary of Henry Sidney and of Lady Warwick, and the letters of Rachel Lady Russell. We have Sir Kenelm Digby's *Private Memoirs*, in which real people are disguised under transparent pseudonyms, and in which his adventures are recorded with a disregard for truth which rendered him the Trelawny of his age. We have Anthony Hamilton's memoirs of his disgraceful brother-in-law the Comte de Gramont, which is so much a work of art that it ceases to be a book of history, and is little more than the first of the *Chroniques Scandaleuses*. We have Evelyn and we have Pepys. And lastly, we have four books which I propose to examine in greater detail since each, in its own way, illustrates distinct phases or aspects in the development of biography.

I shall deal first with the autobiography of Lord Herbert of Cherbury (1583-1648). I shall in general exclude autobiographies from my discussion, but Lord Herbert is so singular that he merits attention. His book, indeed, owing to the almost complete suppression of the known facts of his life in favour of the unknown, of the external in favour of the internal, marks a

Lord Herbert of Cherbury.

THE SEVENTEENTH CENTURY

date. For Lord Herbert was known as a perfectly serious and original philosopher, and as a conscientious, if irritable, diplomatist. Descartes called him "a man above the usual," and Descartes was not given to ready eulogy. Gassendi on reading Lord Herbert's treatise *De Veritate* exclaimed, "O happy England, to have, after losing Verulam, raised up this new hero!" He was admired by Grotius; he was intimate both with Ben Jonson and with Donne. And yet of all these, his serious and ostensible qualities, there is little or nothing in his autobiography. He states that the work contains "those passages of my life which I conceive may best declare me"; and he then proceeds to paint a portrait of a bully and a coxcomb, to relate a catalogue of amatory triumphs and doubtful escapades, and to exhibit himself on every occasion as vain, foolish, blustering, and ridiculous. Herbert's book indicates a surprising departure from the commemorative as well as the didactic tradition; it stands as a model of the unpretentious at the very starting-place of English autobiography. But it is a model that has not been sufficiently regarded.

The seventeenth century, for all its amiable inquisitiveness, possessed no very critical estimate of what in fact constitutes the art of biography. Lady Fanshawe, for instance, was

Lady Fanshawe.

a highly intelligent and cultivated woman. She had a facile pen, a good visual memory, considerable psychological insight, a sense, even, of construction. But in sitting down to write her reminiscences she never considered whether the work was to be a biography of her husband, an autobiography, a book of memoirs, or a diplomatic diary. She begins with all the apparatus of a full-dress biography: there is a moral and didactic exordium, a cenotaph on which are recorded the eminent but wholly unconvincing virtues of Sir Richard Fanshawe. She then passes to the more sprightly style of the memoir, and she degenerates towards the end into the diurnal twaddle of a diplomatic diary. And yet her memoirs possess all the elements of an admirable biography: the synthetic art alone is wanting. She has a fine gift of narrative: the story runs on entertainingly. We have her happy, harum-scarum childhood, when she was a "hoyting girl," though "never immodest but skipping." We have her first meeting with her husband; their early adventures in the congested discomfort of the camp at Oxford; a memorable picture of the troops moving down the road below her as she leant against a tree in the gardens of St. John's College; escapes and adventures; her sufferings in the Scilly Islands; her farewell to Charles I at Hampton Court; her shipwrecks; her brush with a Turkish privateer when she dressed up as the cabin boy; her seeing a ghost in Ireland; her detention under the Commonwealth; her escape on a forged passport; her return to England with Charles II; the Embassy life at Lisbon and Madrid; her husband's recall, his death: and after that the book breaks off in a sudden weariness of disappointment and regret. For had she not, through all this, had fourteen children and six miscarriages? And had not Lord Clarendon behaved unfairly to her husband? Lady Fanshawe can scarcely contain herself when she considers how badly, how despicably, Lord Clarendon had behaved. "So much," she hisses, "are ambassadors slaves to the public ministers at home, who often, through envy or ignorance, ruin them."[1] It was not only that Lord Clarendon did not understand Sir Richard; he was *jealous* of him. It was some comfort to Lady Fanshawe to reflect how acutely jealous the Chancellor had been.

The particular charm of Lady Fanshawe's memoirs is largely adventitious, and is found in the books of other widow-biographers. Lady Fanshawe, however, has more serious claims to our attention.

---

[1] *Memoirs of Lady Fanshawe*, edited by Beatrice Marshall (John Lane, 1905), p. 20.

Although her book is faultily constructed, although she is delightfully inaccurate about dates and names and places, yet she really did endeavour to give a certain unity of impression and correctly to convey the atmosphere of her age. In this she is abundantly successful. Although her book abounds in digressions and is marred by breaks in continuity, yet its "values" are uniformly correct. She set out to tell the story "of honest, worthy and virtuous men and women, who served God in their generations in their several capacities, and without vanity, none excelled them in loyalty which cost them dear."[1] And in spite of her shrewd and adventurous gaiety, her sometimes passionate bias; in spite of the fact that, in many respects, she remained a "hoyting girl" to the end, yet the whole tone of the book accurately reflects the severe colour of her age, a devout and serious endurance, a sincere conviction that black was indeed black and that white was white.

A similar certainty of outlook inspires and invalidates Mrs. Hutchinson's memoirs of her husband, a work written between 1664 and 1671. To Lucy Hutchinson the Royalist party were simply "the ungodly," or the "debauchees."

Mrs. Hutchinson.

[1] *Memoirs of Lady Fanshawe*, edited by Beatrice Marshall (John Lane, 1905), p. 49.

THE SEVENTEENTH CENTURY

She speaks continually of "*their* darkness and *our* light." She is not an attractive woman. In later life an ill-dressed blue stocking, she must even as a girl have been almost intolerable. She dwells with irritating complacency on her early education, on her prowess in Latin, on the fact that "play among other children I despised." She calls her book "a naked undressed narrative"; but it is in fact somewhat pretentious, and is marred by digressions and rhetoric. She defines her husband's life as "nothing else but a progress from one degree of virtue to another." She then proceeds to catalogue these virtues, and the result is a flat and uninteresting monochrome of adulation. Here again we have the widow-biographer ascribing her husband's lack of ultimate success to Cromwell's jealousy. "But now," she writes ("now" was a stage at which Colonel Hutchinson, being a prominent regicide, expected some signal promotion), "the poison of ambition so ulcerated Cromwell's heart that the effects of it became more apparent than before. . . . He was moulding the army to his mind, weeding out the godly and filling up their room with rascally turn-coat cavaliers and pitiful sottish beasts of his own alliance."[1] No, Mrs. Hutchinson is not an

[1] *Memoirs of Colonel Hutchinson*, by Lucy Hutchinson, 1906 edition (George Bell & Son), p. 342.

attractive writer; she represents the widow-biographer at her very worst.

I turn with pleasure from Mrs. Hutchinson to a personality of infinitely greater charm and original-**The Duchess of Newcastle.** ity. The Duchess of Newcastle's biography of her husband, together with her memoir of herself, are published in the Everyman edition, and should most assuredly be read. The praises lavished on her by Charles Lamb, the more recent appreciation which figures in *The Common Reader* of Virginia Woolf, are both fully merited, since the Duchess of Newcastle possessed a mind startlingly active and original. Her biography of her husband, which was published during the poor man's lifetime, is perhaps less successful than the companion volume of her own reminiscences. In the former her style was cramped by the Duke's refusal to permit her to abuse his enemies. It is cramped also by the practical difficulty of explaining away his very equivocal behaviour during the Civil War. She is kind about him, since they were evidently devoted. "He was the only person," she wrote later, "I ever was in love with: neither was I ashamed to own it, but gloried therein. For it was not amorous love, I never was infected therewith: it is a disease, or a passion or both, I only know by relation, not by experience. But my love

THE SEVENTEENTH CENTURY

was honest and honourable."[1] And so she makes the best of the Duke. As a general, she says (somewhat vaguely), he was every bit as good as Cæsar; as a man, she compared him to "Titus, the Deliciæ of Mankind, by reason of his sweet, gentle, and obliging nature."[2] And yet—"My Lord naturally loves not business, especially those of the State." And yet—"He is neat and cleanly: which makes him to be somewhat long in dressing." For with the Duchess of Newcastle truth will out. She was the first of those few but estimable writers whose love of truth triumphs over all caution and all modesty. The latter quality, it must be admitted, was not one of the more salient traits in the Duchess's character. "It pleased God," she writes, "to command His servant Nature to indulge me with a poetical and philosophical genius, even from my birth."[3] "I have heard," she writes again, "that some should say my wit seemed as if it would overpower my brain."[4] And it is with the following apology that she concludes her memoir on herself:—

But I hope my readers will not think me vain for writing my life, since there have been many that have

---

[1] *Memoirs of Duchess of Newcastle*, Everyman edition, p. 185.
[2] *Life of Duke of Newcastle*, Everyman edition, p. 138.
[3] *Memoirs of Duchess of Newcastle*, Everyman edition, p. 5.
[4] *Ibid.*, p. 181.

done the like as Cæsar, Ovid, and many more both men and women, and I know no reason I may not do it as well as they. . . . 'Tis no purpose to the readers, but it is to the authoress, because I write it for my own sake, not theirs: neither did I intend this piece for to delight, but to divulge: not to please the fancy, but to tell the truth, for after ages should mistake, in not knowing I was daughter to Master Lucas of St. John's, near Colchester, in Essex, second wife to the Lord Marquis of Newcastle: for my Lord having had two wives, I might easily have been mistaken, especially if I should dye and my Lord marry again.[1]

It is not, I think, very intelligent to dismiss the Duchess of Newcastle merely as an example of morbid egoism. Her curiosity, her zest, her frankness amount to genius; her energy is a mountain torrent carrying accuracy and caution as straws before it. She admits her inaccuracy and her impulsiveness. "I must also acknowledge," she writes, "that I have committed great errors in taking no notion of times (dates) as I should have done in many places of this history."[2] "For besides," she writes again, "that I want also that skill of scholarship and true writing, I did many times not peruse the copies that were transcribed, lest they should disturb my following conceptions. By which neglect, as I said, many errors are slipt into my books."[3]

[1] *Memoirs of Duchess of Newcastle*, Everyman edition, p. 213.
[2] *Life of Duke of Newcastle*, Everyman edition, p. 17.
[3] *Dedication*, Everyman edition, p. 7.

THE SEVENTEENTH CENTURY

Such frankness, such transparent and energetic honesty, render her the true precursor of Mrs. Asquith. She was eccentric, doubtless; she dressed extravagantly and "in such fashion as I did invent myself." On the rare occasions when she came to London in her black and silver coach she was "followed and crowded upon all the way she went." (I quote from Pepys.) She wrote a vast number of philosophical treatises on subjects which she was incapable of understanding; and she evidently made several enemies owing to her mistaken impression that other people relished frankness as much as she did herself. But there was nothing small or cautious about her, nothing mean. "I am a great emulator," she exclaims magnificently. "My ambition," she says again, "inclines to vainglory, for I am very ambitious: yet 'tis neither for beauty, wit, titles, wealth or power, but as they are steps to raise me to Fame's tower, which is to live by remembrance in after ages." [1]

The Duchess of Newcastle has had her desire.

[1] *Memoirs of Duchess of Newcastle,* Everyman edition, p. 211.

III

FROM WALTON TO JOHNSON, 1670-1780

Limitations of seventeenth-century biography—Walton's *Lives*—Sprat's *Cowley*—Dryden—Eighteenth-century biography—Colley Cibber—North—The Newgate Calendar—Mason's *Gray*—Dr. Johnson—His theory—His practice.

IN my previous lecture I showed how the main current of English biography tended, during the **Limitations of** seventeenth century, to run into sub-**seventeenth-** sidiary channels; how it was tapped **century** **biography.** by history, by the character-sketch, and by memoirs. The essential cause of this was, I suggest, the moral earnestness of the time. The devout, as Dean Stanley has so convincingly demonstrated, are not gifted with a genius for biography; their preoccupation with theology and the life after death somewhat blurs their interest in man, and in the life that is ours, and theirs, upon this varied earth. For biography is essentially a profane brand of literature; its triumphs do not proceed from theological convictions. We shall see this same moral earnestness cramping biography in 1840. We shall see its reverse liberating biography

FROM WALTON TO JOHNSON

in 1780 and again in 1907. For biography is the preoccupation and the solace, not of certainty but of doubt. And during our Puritan periods English biography declines.

It is thus with Izaak Walton. His *Lives* of Wotton, Herbert, and the rest are, I am assured, literary masterpieces: they are beautifully constructed, beautifully balanced; their style is tranquil and limpid; they constitute delightful essays on the charms of studious quiet, on the fretting illusions of active ambition. They are unquestionably works of art; but are they unquestionably pure biography? Where Walton fails is in truth: he fails to present us with complete or even probable portraits; the intrusion of his own feelings and predilections is too apparent; he is too confident of his own ethical values; he surrenders too readily to the deductive method. For Walton, as we know, was actually obsessed by the fascination of doing nothing. He was interested only in those sides of character which reflected his own negative and receptive temperament. His bias is always in favour of calm and caution and devout scholarship, of that "grave behaviour" which he calls "a divine charm." And thus, in dealing with a singularly mundane diplomatist like Wotton, or with a tortured sensualist

Walton's "Lives."

like Donne, Walton very flagrantly misleads. And yet Walton, to a not inconsiderable degree, was a pioneer. He was our first *deliberate* biographer. He was the first to write biography with intention rather than by accident. He possessed also many qualities which, until his day, had not been consciously united in the art of biography. He had a sense of reverence, but it did not blind him; he had charity, but it did not render him dull or merely adulatory; he had accuracy, but it did not tempt him to be pedantic. His sincerity is absolute; his modesty is charming. "Though I cannot," he writes, "adorn it with eloquence yet I will do it with sincerity." He has a real gift for intimacy, and is clearly ill at ease when, as in his *Life of Hooker*, he is unable to convey that sense of intimacy in the presentation of which, in his other biographies, he has taken such obvious delight. How often, for instance, does he convey a touch of gentle familiarity by the introduction of some affectionate possessive: "He proceeded to his dear Kent"; or again, "His dear Edwin Sandys and his as dear George Cranmer." Then Walton was humorous. It is difficult to believe that the story of Hooker's marriage to his landlady's daughter, and of his subsequent exploitation by that young lady, was due merely to Izaak's affection for unworldliness. For Izaak, on occasions, could be sly. We hear of Andrew Melville, when confined to the Tower, remaining "very angry for three years"; the impulsiveness of George Herbert, his marriage and his induction to the living of Bemerton, are described without comment but with obviously conscious humour; and we have the following dig at Mrs. Herbert: "Jane became so much a Platonick as to fall in love with Mr. Herbert unseen." A touch, here, almost of Mr. Lytton Strachey. Although, moreover, his *Lives* were written at widely different periods between 1640 and 1678, yet they are all given the same deliberate shape and construction: the digressions, when they occur, occur at suitable pauses in the dramatic narrative; they are frequently due, as is the introduction of Sir A. Morton and Mr. Bedell into the final pages of the *Life of Wotton*, to mere civility. For Walton was a kindly man, and Mr. Bedell, who was difficult to fit in, would have been deeply offended had he not been fitted in at all. It is in fact this kindliness, this gentleness of Izaak Walton, which mar his book. "The feather," exclaimed Wordsworth:

> The feather, whence the pen
> Was shaped that traced the lives of these good men,
> Dropped from an Angel's wing. With moistened eyes, . . .

This is all very well, but we get a little tired of Walton's frequent use of such expressions as "sweet content" and "sweet tranquillity"; with his passion for meekness; with his suppression of what were in fact the violent and essential parts of the earlier George Herbert no less than of the earlier Donne. For by painting every one in watercolour Walton failed to give relief to his characters. They are all flat and uniform: and we may be certain that neither the real Donne, nor the real Wotton, nor the real Herbert resembled one another in the least. There is a further criticism which I would make against Walton: he has no insight into fact; he has no interest in practical activity; he has no sense of actuality. He wrote of Wotton as of a fishing friend, but he was far more interested in him as Provost of Eton than as the man who scribbled that unfortunate sentence in the Augsburg album. He wrote of the gentle and pious Vicar of Bemerton, but did he ever understand that George Herbert also composed poems of the very highest secular value? "He sang on earth," he writes, "such Hymns and Anthems as the Angels and he and Mr. Farrer now sing in heaven." Surely an inadequate appreciation of our greatest religious poet before Christina Rossetti? Such strictures

FROM WALTON TO JOHNSON

may be captious. Izaak Walton was the first Englishman consciously to write artistic biography. It was he, and not Mason, who revived Eadmer's admirable practice of introducing original letters into the text. It was he also who first adopted the more questionable procedure of enlivening his narrative with imaginary conversations. His immediate influence, moreover, was considerable: his book went into four editions between 1670 and 1675. It is certainly the most important biographical work in English literature prior to Johnson.

One cannot say less of Walton; there are doubtless many enthusiasts who would say much more.

<small>Sprat's "Cowley," 1668.</small> My prejudice against him (and I admit a prejudice) is due to the fact that he represents a reversion to hagiography; that his book is the prototype of many idyllic biographies of which the best is Carlyle's *Sterling* and of which the worst are too bad to name. If Walton, however, exaggerates the lyrical element in biography, Thomas Sprat errs in the opposite direction. He is so objective as to become wholly impersonal; his biography of *Cowley* is as cold as any cenotaph, as stilted as any obituary. It is cast in the form of a letter addressed to Mr. Clifford, and is in truth a deplorable production. I mention it

only because it stands as the originator and model of a form of biography which flourished in the first half of the seventeenth century, and to which the Victorians for their part turned with complacent delight. For Dr. Sprat abandoned the tradition of Aubrey, the tradition even of Walton. He adhered to the tradition of Jeremy Taylor, who, although perhaps "the Shakespeare of English prose," was, as a biographer, formal, superficial, and unctuously insincere. Sprat, who with his contemporaries had all the authority of a pundit, is important as being the originator of the pernicious theory that it is indelicate to publish private letters in a biography. He was attacked by Johnson, he was attacked by Coleridge; but the tradition of "discreet" biography owes its wretched origin to him.

Dryden could have countered this influence, but Dryden was busy with other things. Such references as he makes to biography are uniformly intelligent. In 1683 he prefaced an edition of *Plutarch* with an Introduction in which the actual word "biography" first occurs in English, and is defined as "the history of particular men's lives." While admitting that biography is necessarily inferior in "dignity" to the cognate art of history, he yet contends that the "pleasure

Dryden.

and instruction . . . the perfection of the work and the benefit arising from it are both more absolute in biography than in history." "The pageantry of life," he writes, "is taken away: you see the poor reasonable animal as naked as ever nature made him: are made acquainted with his passions and his follies: and find the demi-god a man."

This, however, was exactly what one did not find until Johnson. Sprat conquered Dryden. Such works as Gilbert Burnet's *Life of William Bedell* (1685), or Bishop Hacket's *Scrinia Reserata* (1695) —those 458 folio pages of discourse about the Lord Keeper Williams—are not readable biographies. With the early eighteenth century biography became even more artificial and rhetorical; for a few years the interest in it declined. People looked to the drama for their enjoyment, and when the drama palled they had Swift and Steele and Addison, and eventually the novel. Inevitably the essay on contemporary manners, the novel of contemporary life, exercised a powerful and durable effect upon the development of English biography. They revived our national talent for realism, they gave an important stimulus to curiosity and sympathy, they created a habit of psychological observation, they enormously increased the numbers of the reading public, and they gave that public a very definite taste for detail. It would be a mistake, therefore, to assume that the absence during the first forty years of the eighteenth century of any important biography, except that of Roger North, indicates any interruption in the development of the art itself. The gap between Sprat and Mason is a wide one, but in the interval the art of biography had developed underground, had thrust out sturdy roots and sensitive fibres through which it obtained the sustenance of new and richer soil. Sprat's *Cowley* dates from 1668; Johnson's *Life of Savage* from 1744; Mason's *Gray* from 1774; Johnson's *Lives of the Poets* from 1777-80. Johnson was one of the greatest figures in our literature; but Mason was not a genius, and the excellence of his biography of *Gray* is due not to any phenomenal originality on his part, but to obscure developments in the art of biography itself. The primary influence in such developments was, as I have said, the essay and the novel; the second was the growth of the coffeehouse, the stimulus thereby given to gossip and conversation. For biography is an essentially "clubbable" art. A third influence was the spread of education and the increasing knowledge of French literature. We must also take into account the sense of freedom engendered by greater political security and greater religious tolerance; the gradual decline in feudal reverence and religious preoccupation; the increasing importance, interest, and self-confidence of the average educated man.

The fact remains, however, that the first forty years of the eighteenth century produced little of any biographical value. There is William Oldys' *Life of Raleigh* in 1736, and his contribution to the *Biographica Britannica* of 1747-60; but Oldys, who was little more than an antiquarian, stands, for what he is worth, almost alone. We find nothing of importance until we reach Colley Cibber's *Apology for his Life*, which dates from 1740. This sprightly volume is invaluable to those who care for theatrical anecdotes, and is useful also to more serious students of the English stage. It gives a vivid and convincing narrative of the difficulties, the jealousies, and the intrigues which affected the English stage between 1690 and 1730. But I for one am in no sense deeply interested in the rivalry between the Haymarket and the Drury Lane Theatres, nor am I anxious to learn all that can be learnt about Mr. Nokes, Mr. Underhill, and Mr. Leigh. The book, moreover, in spite of its naïf and confidential tone, gives us no convincing portrait of

[margin: Colley Cibber.]

the author. It is intolerably diffuse, intolerably conceited. One is left wondering how any one so foolish as Colley Cibber could even in a momentary fit of irritation have been taken seriously by Pope.

Far more important than Cibber is Roger North, whose biographies of his three brothers, although written about 1715, were only published between 1740 and 1744. This entertaining collection is entirely in the manner of Aubrey, not in the least in the manner of Dr. Sprat or even of Walton. For Roger North was out to tell the truth. He tells it racily, inaccurately, vividly, and in a slangy, conversational style. He introduces letters and memoranda as being "images of interior thought." "I fancy myself," he writes, "as a picture-drawer, and aiming to give the same picture to a spectator as I had of the thing itself." His style, he says, is not intended to be "polite"; "if it be significant, it is well." And the style of Roger North is highly significant, whether he be writing of Francis North—"my best brother"—that ambitious lawyer, whose only lapse from decorum was when, as Lord Chief Justice, he climbed, out of curiosity, upon the back of the rhinoceros; or of that other brother, Sir Dudley North, the gay merchant adventurer, who visited Archangel and Smyrna, and who lived for years at Constantinople amassing a large fortune and much experience, both of which he subsequently lavished in his own country and on his own diversions. Or again of that third less fortunate brother, Dr. John North, whose features were those of a "Madam *en travestie*," whose walk was "weak and shuffling, often crossing his legs as if he were tipsy"; who, thus endowed, became Master of Trinity, and was so frightened at night that "when he was in bed alone he durst not trust his countenance above the clothes"; who kept tame spiders in glass jars; and who, while admonishing two undergraduates, was struck with the palsy, "whereafter there was a prodigious declination of the doctor's mind to levities." Poor Dr. North, these levities were not very inspiriting! They took the form of sherry, and again more sherry, after which he would get some undergraduates up to the Lodge, and would make them tell smutty stories, at which he laughed immoderately—"but (as his visage was then distorted) most deformly." And then he died, and his younger brother, some fifteen years later, wrote the gay and vivid biography by which he has been immortalised. For Roger North deserves a very high place in the history of English biography. In an age of seriousness he wrote with humour, frankness, and great graphic and dramatic skill. It is he, far more than Mason, who links the "actuality" of Aubrey with the "actuality" of Boswell.

North shows us that in spite of appearances there existed a really healthy taste for biography in the early eighteenth century. This taste was stimulated by the democratisation of biography which took place at the same time. There arose a sudden interest in the lives of the obscure. As early as 1714 Captain Alexander Smith wrote his *History of the Lives of the most Noted Highwaymen, Footpads, Housebreakers, Shoplifters, Etc.* Edmund Curll, so quick to catch the breeze of public interest, thereafter published as many as fifty scurrilous biographies of eminent or notorious persons. Defoe between 1722 and 1725 wrote several biographies of criminals, of Jack Sheppard and Jonathan Wild. We had the Newgate Calendar; we had the Grub Street school. "These books," writes Professor Walter Raleigh, "commanded a large sale, and modern biography was established."

The Newgate Calendar.

It was thus on a world not wholly unprepared for such a portent that Johnson's *Life of Savage* broke in 1744. This unquestionably is our first masterpiece in biography, but at the moment it passed almost unnoticed. It was not

Mason's "Gray."

till it was republished with the other Lives (1777-80) that the genius of Johnson as a biographer was generally recognised. I shall therefore postpone the *Life of Savage* till I can deal with it in discussing Johnson's work as a whole. I shall first speak of Mason's *Life of Gray,* which exercised an important influence both on Boswell and on Johnson himself, and which is the first biography deliberately written on the "life-and-letters" method. Walton, it is true, had introduced letters into some of his biographies, but he had done so with no very deliberate purpose. Mason's purpose was deliberate and avowed. He is said to have first conceived of this method on reading Middleton's *Cicero;* but he expanded it, and allowed the letters to tell their own story, introducing them only with short explanatory captions, or explaining them by sensible and vivid notes. "In a word," as he says, "Mr. Gray will become his own biographer."[1]

But Mason has his faults. In the first place, as can be seen from the Rev. John Mitford's edition of 1853, he played tricks with his text. We do not commit such crimes today. We do not alter the text; we merely leave out the bits that contradict our own thesis. But Mason actually falsified the written word, which is indefensible. In the second

[1] Mason's *Gray,* edition of 1820, p. 9.

place, Mason allowed his friendly feelings towards Gray to blur his sincerity. Johnson himself criticises this aspect of Skroddles Mason—"whose fondness and fidelity has kindled in him a zeal of admiration which cannot be reasonably expected from the neutrality of a stranger and the coldness of a critic." And in the third place, Mason's prejudices and jealousies obtrude. He makes no mention of Bonstetten, who was certainly the central and most illuminating factor in Gray's life. He is jealous of all Gray's own friends, with the possible exception of Walpole. And he suppressed all unfavourable references to Tories, while inserting all eulogies of the Whigs. In spite of these faults, and in addition to the all-important innovation which he introduced, Mason is a sensible and honest biographer. Above all, he was fully conscious of what he was about. "I am well aware," he notes when first reproducing one of Gray's letters, "that I am here going to do a thing which the cautious and courtly Dr. Sprat (were he now alive) would highly censure."[1] "The method," he writes again, "in which I have arranged the foregoing pages has, I trust, one degree of merit—that it makes the reader so well acquainted with the man himself as to render it totally unnecessary to conclude the whole with his char-

[1] Mason's *Gray*, edition of 1820, note on p. 8.

acter. . . . I might have written his life in the common form, perhaps with more reputation to myself, but surely not with equal information to the reader."[1] You will observe the importance of this passage. Not only did Mason invent a new method and one far more important than he himself perhaps realised, but he was conscious that this new method possessed a subtle literary value: it definitely enlisted the co-operation of the reader; it deliberately threw upon the latter the onus of drawing his own conclusions.

This, indubitably, marked a great advance, an important enlargement of the potential area and scope of biography. The implications of Mason's discovery were not, as I have said, realised at the time. Mason was little more than one of several country parsons who were interested in literature. His book was widely read, but he possessed small literary authority, and had it not been for its influence on Boswell, the *Life of Gray* might well have remained unnoticed. Mason, almost by chance, hit upon a method which rendered possible the technique of biography as we know it today. But it is Dr. Johnson who is the real founder of pure biography, for he was the first to proclaim that biography was a distinct branch of

[1] Mason's *Gray*, edition of 1820, p. 400.

creative literature. Mason merely showed people how to do it; Johnson showed people that it was a highly interesting and important thing to do. For Johnson, with his mistrust of history and his dislike of fiction, found in biography a satisfaction such as no other branch of literature could provide. Johnson was in no sense drugged by his own religious convictions. He laboured in doubt. His terror of death, his basic incredulity about life after death, gave him a deeply personal interest in mundane life, induced him to interest himself in the personal and the humane with an almost terrified intensity. And being a man of intelligence as well as a man of letters, he was not content until he had worked out his own theory of why human life interested him so deeply, and of what were the purposes and objects which biography should serve. Evidences of his constant preoccupation with the theory of biography can be found in many of his writings and in very many of his recorded remarks. His observations, when collected together, constitute perhaps the best definition of biography as an art which has yet been formulated. I propose to examine them in some detail.

In the *Rambler* for 13th October 1750[1] we have the first extended statement of Dr. Johnson's views. He begins by saying that the interest of any given biography lies in "the

His theory.

[1] *Rambler*, No. 60.

parallel circumstances and kindred images to which we readily conform our minds." In history this interest is blurred and diffused; in biography it is concentrated. Dr. Johnson feels, moreover, that the biography of almost any individual would be worth writing provided only that it were ably and vividly composed. He contends that it is a mistake to imagine, as most of his contemporaries imagined, that a biography must necessarily deal with exciting adventures or important public events. On the contrary, the art of the biographer is to "pass slightly over those performances and incidents which produce vulgar greatness, to lead the thoughts into domestic privacies, and to display the minute details of daily life." With this in mind he condemns the "formal and studied narrative" which begins with a man's pedigree and ends with his funeral; he inveighs against the arbitrary introduction of "striking or wonderful vicissitudes"; he asks only for truth, for vivid detail, for psychological insight. This brings him to the problem of the ethics of biography, to the incessant conflict between truth and loyalty, between the portrait and the obituary notice. Of this problem also he disposes with courage and good sense. "There are many," he writes, "who think it an act of piety to hide the faults or failings of their friends, even when they can no longer suffer by their detection. We therefore see whole ranks of characters adorned with uniform panegyric, and not to be known from one another but by extrinsic and casual circumstances." "If," concludes Dr. Johnson, "we owe regard to the memory of the dead, there is yet more respect to be laid to knowledge, to virtue, and to truth." This admirable article is supplemented by another written over nine years later.[1] In this Dr. Johnson begins by contending that biography, as lying midway between the "falsehood" of fiction and the "useless truth" of history, is "of the various kinds of narrative writing that which is most eagerly read and more easily applied to the purposes of life." The essential of good biography is truth. To obtain truth one must have that "certainty of knowledge" which "not only excludes mistakes but fortifies veracity." "I esteem biography," he remarked, "as giving us what comes near to ourselves, what we can turn to use. . . ."[2] Or again: "The value of every story depends on its being true. A story is a picture either of an individual or of human nature in general. If it is false, it is a picture of nothing."[3] To Dr. Johnson the whole interest of a biography thus centred is its truth. On one oc-

[1] *Idler*, No. 84, 24th November 1759.
[2] *Journal of a Tour to the Hebrides*, Everyman edition, p. 63.
[3] Boswell's *Life*, Everyman edition, vol. i, p. 609.

casion he told Mrs. Thrale that a true story was to him "an idea the more." This remark, if properly considered, not only is profound in itself, but explains Johnson's essential attitude towards the art which he was the first man of letters deliberately to isolate and exploit.

His passion for candour, his detestation of all forms of cant, are implicit in all his biographies, and are rendered all the more effective from the good sense of most of his remarks on character and conduct. When Johnson was silly (as about America) he blundered and blustered like Leviathan. But in general (and we are apt to forget it) Johnson was far from silly. He was acute. Take, for instance, his remarks on Milton as a schoolmaster; his trenchant criticism of Oldisworth's character of Edmund Smith (a character which, "without criminal purpose of deceiving, shows a strong desire to make the most of all favourable truth");[1] or his admirable attack on Prior's pose of liking low company. Scarcely less important than his candour was his passionate interest in the psychology of individuals. He had little taste for the Theophrastian character, although he had essayed it in some of his papers for the

His practice.

[1] Johnson's *Lives of the Poets*, Everyman edition, vol. i, p. 288.

Rambler and the *Idler*. What really interested him were the strange manifestations, not of typical but of individual character. He was occupied, and this is his vital contribution to biography, not with externals but with internals. "A blade of grass," he said to Mrs. Thrale, "is always a blade of grass: men and women are *my* subjects of inquiry."[1] "Besides," he said to Boswell at Edinburgh, "I love anecdotes." His curiosity, indeed, was insatiable, his observation acute, his analysis masterly. He never accepted a given quality at its face value; he always examined it, turned it over, estimated its relation to other qualities and defects, rendered it with all its light and shade. He was not one of those who imagine sentimentally that a writer is best known by his books. Johnson wished always to interpret the works by the writer's character and the details of his ascertainable experience. We thus have such admirable passages of analysis as the examination of the relations between Steele and Addison, the inquiry regarding the exact quality of the latter's bashfulness, the detailed record of Pope's habits and affectations, the portrait of Savage, the lights and shadows of his feckless optimism and his ruthless indiscretion. We have vivid pictures, such as that of Addison during the first performance of

[1] Mrs. Piozzi's *Anecdotes*, 1786 edition, p. 100.

Cato wandering "through the whole exhibition behind the scenes with restless and unappeasable solicitude";[1] of Savage reading his own verses and from time to time "stealing his eyes from the page to discover in the faces of his audience how they were affected with any favourite passage";[2] of Gay upsetting a Japanese screen when about to read *The Captives* to the Princess of Wales.[3] And all this conceived and moulded as a work of literary art; the narrative and the criticism being cast in a style of the most compelling lucidity and force, and enlivened by sullen flashes of irony and epigram. It is true that the critical portions of the *Lives of the Poets* may dismay the sensitive; the biographical portions, however, cannot fail to charm. For they are, in the words of Lord Rosebery, "the work of a master of letters dealing with the department of literature which he loved the best."

Yet it is not merely their charm which renders Johnson's *Lives of the Poets* an all-important factor in the development of English biography. It is the circumstance that the leading literary figure of his age should have set himself to write a series of

---

[1] Johnson's *Lives of the Poets*, Everyman edition, vol. i, p. 338.
[2] *Ibid.*, vol. ii, p. 140.
[3] *Ibid.*, p. 38.

biographies conceived as works of art; that he should have composed these biographies with the determination to tell the truth completely and courageously; and that he should have brought to their composition what Mr. Lytton Strachey has called his "immovable independence of thought—his searching sense of actuality."

IV

THE BOSWELL FORMULA, 1791

The Boswell legend—His charm—His self-abasement—His humour—His opportunity—Sir John Hawkins—Mrs. Thrale—His actual achievement—Quality of his intelligence—His literary gifts—His originality—His courage.

I ENDED my last lecture with the word "actuality." It is with the same word that I should wish to begin my study of the Boswell formula. For James Boswell invented actuality; he discovered and perfected a biographical formula in which the narrative could be fused with the pictorial, in which the pictorial in its turn could be rendered in a series of photographs so vividly, and above all so rapidly, projected as to convey an impression of continuity, of progression—in a word, of life. Previous biographers had composed a studio portrait, or at best a succession of lantern slides. Boswell's method was that of the cinematograph. In perfecting his experiment he showed singular originality and surprising courage. He well deserves the central position which he and his formula must always occupy. But the problem of Boswell can-

The Boswell legend.

not be elucidated solely by the appreciative method. We must dissect and isolate; we must begin by isolating Boswell from his own legend; then, and then only, will it be possible to define what exactly was his contribution to the art of English biography.

The problem which has puzzled so many critics from Macaulay to Mr. Birrell is how a man so palpably silly as Boswell could have written what is rightly regarded as the greatest of English biographies. I question whether there does not exist some confusion between the emotional and the intellectual responses which his work excites; between its charm on the one hand and its value on the other. I should be the last to deny that the *Life of Johnson* is, as Boswell himself remarked, "the most entertaining book that ever appeared." But how far is this entertainment legitimate? How can we meet the criticism that it arises only from the accident that the book was written *by* Boswell and *about* Johnson; was written, that is, about a highly alarming eccentric by a singularly observant buffoon?

His charm.

Let us first examine this business about Boswell's "charm." It will be found, I think, that it rests on a somewhat fragile basis, and that our ready acceptance of it is due largely

His self-abasement.

THE BOSWELL FORMULA

to the circumstance that his constant self-abasement flatters our own self-esteem. We think of him as "lovable" because of the fictitious intimacy which his book conveys. I use the word "fictitious" advisedly, since we approach Boswell as a "character," and as a "character" in a novel—as a delightfully exaggerated type of certain laughable human frailties. But had we actually known Boswell we should have sympathised acutely with the irritated despair of old Lord Auchinleck, with the ashamed reticence of Sir Alexander Boswell, the biographer's reputable and scholarly son. For Boswell was a drunkard, and of the whining, good-resolution type. His sensuality was of a sort which it is difficult to regard as charming. Nor can one view without disgust his flabby dalliance with trulls and parlour-maids, his shifty unfaithfulness to his wife when living, his maudlin self-pity and self-reproach when she was dead. His egoism also is insufferable. "Boswell," thundered Johnson on one occasion, "you often vaunt so much as to provoke ridicule." That Boswell should himself have recorded such well-merited rebukes is often regarded as highly creditable to his frankness and as a singularly endearing procedure. Such apologies for Boswell as have been attempted have generally been based on the argument that there is nothing we can say against Boswell which he does not admit against himself. In other words, whatever Boswell may have been he was not a hypocrite; his frankness of self-disclosure is regarded as covering the multitude of his sins. But does this excuse really describe Boswell's method of self-revelation? There is a passage in the *Life* in which, with his usual incapacity for retention, he, even on this point, gives himself away. They were discussing the French *ana*, and had apparently passed on to autobiography. "A man," said Johnson, "cannot with propriety speak of himself, except he relates simple facts; as, 'I was at Richmond'; or, what depends on mensuration; 'I am six feet high.' He is sure that he has been at Richmond; he is sure he is six feet high; but he cannot be sure he is wise, or that he has any other excellence. Then, all censure of a man's self is oblique praise. It is in order to show how much he can spare. It has all the invidiousness of self-praise and all the reproach of falsehood." [Boswell]—"Sometimes it may proceed from a man's strong consciousness of his faults being observed. He knows that others would throw him down, and therefore that he had better lie down softly of his own accord."[1] I am not myself moved by the spectacle of a grown man

[1] Boswell's *Life of Johnson*, Everyman edition, vol. ii, p. 231.

THE BOSWELL FORMULA

lying on his back like a puppy, paws in air, trusting to the humble exposure of his most tender parts to "disarm" castigation. For this indeed was Boswell's method of defence. He had a very acute "consciousness of his faults being observed." He deliberately set out, therefore, to forestall criticism by lying down "softly of his own accord." He thus narrates his several discomfitures and humiliations lest others might do so for him: he speaks (with but half frankness) of his drunkenness and his lechery; he tells without quailing that awful story of the evening party at Inveraray, that still more awful story of his dinner with the Duke of Montrose; he describes, for instance, how nearly he was black-balled for the club, or what a fool he made of himself that other evening by giving farmyard imitations from the pit at Drury Lane. There are some, perhaps, who will regard all this as an indication of Bozzy's endearing simplicity. I regard it myself as an instance of sly self-defence at the expense of average human dignity.

A further constituent of Boswell's "charm" is his treatment of the ludicrous. His apologists would contend that he possessed a very delicate sense of humour, and that he displays consummate literary tact in refraining from

His humour.

all comment on the grotesque situations which he so frequently records. This, I think, is an incorrect assumption. A sense of humour was not usual in the eighteenth century, which was concerned rather with wit. It is true that Boswell seldom misses the point of a story; but the point of Dr. Johnson's stories were, like the point of a pickaxe, exceedingly difficult to miss. I should be the last to deny also that Boswell had a very gay appreciation of wit. I would admit further, that he was dimly aware that the juxtaposition, in Johnson's personality, of the venerable and the grotesque was provocative of mirth. But I do not think that he had any intelligent perception of why he sometimes felt inclined to unseasonable laughter, or that his appreciation of the ludicrous was more subtle than the giggling irreverence of a boy at a private school. It is in fact fallacious to attribute to Boswell qualities of humour which we ourselves can extract from his books, but which he, in fact, did not possess. Mrs. Thrale, for instance, had a far more sensitive appreciation of the comic. Yet even Mrs. Thrale, even Fanny Burney, were so blinded by their reverence for Johnson's wit that they were unconscious of his humour. The only recorded instance when Dr. Johnson really got the worst of it is given us by Mrs. Thrale, and is given us with a comment

THE BOSWELL FORMULA

of disapproval. I quote the passage, since it is little known:

> The roughness of the language used on board a man-of-war when he (Dr. Johnson) passed a week on a visit to Captain Knight, disgusted him terribly. He asked an officer what some place was called, and received for answer that it was where the loplolly man kept his loplolly: a reply he considered, not unjustly, as disrespectful, gross and ignorant.[1]

Mrs. Thrale was a woman of exceptional vivacity and penetration. Her attitude to Dr. Johnson was far more "intelligent" than that of Boswell. Yet she can record the above story not only without a smile but with a frown of disapproval. It is unreasonable to expect from Boswell a sense of humour greater than that of Mrs. Thrale, who was far more advanced and intellectual than he. Nor would Boswell have allowed himself consciously to make a sport of Johnson. The few occasions when he permitted himself to do so were branded in hot scars upon his memory. He had laughed once at Johnson's nightcap. "This comes," thundered the Doctor, "of being a little wrong-headed." He had laughed once (and this time "immoderately") when Dr. Johnson said that if he possessed a seraglio he would dress all the ladies in linen. On which there

[1] Mrs. Piozzi's (Mrs. Thrale's) *Anecdotes of Dr. Johnson*, 1786 edition, p. 285.

descended upon Boswell a volley of such "degrading images, of every one of which I was the object, that, though I can bear such attacks as well as most men, I yet found myself so much the sport of all the company, that I would gladly expunge from my mind every trace of this severe retort."[1]

I think it is important thus to isolate the accretion of "charm" which obscures the bones of Boswell's biography. It is a mistake to confuse charm with value; to confuse the amount of pleasure which we get out of the *Life* and the *Journal* with the amount of literary talent which Boswell put into them. It is only when we realise that Boswell's self-abasement was scarcely admirable, and that his so-called sense of humour is an anachronism imported into his work by ourselves, that we can examine his volumes from the critical rather than the sentimental point of view. If we decide to forget or to deny that Boswell was "lovable," we can then proceed, freed of all affectionate bias, to consider how great an artist Boswell really was.

Before we do this, however, we must proceed to a further process of isolation. Having segregated Boswell from his charm, we must segregate him from his opportunity. For his amazing good fortune in having Johnson as a sub-

His opportunity.

[1] *Journal of a Tour to the Hebrides*, Everyman edition, p. 110.

THE BOSWELL FORMULA

ject is essentially an external factor, and has little to do with the quality of Boswell's mind or talent.

The first step is to examine Boswell's capacity when he is not writing about Johnson. The second is to examine Johnsoniana as written by people other than Boswell. These examinations disclose that, until Boswell began to write about Johnson, he never evolved his own formula; and that other people, when writing about Johnson, wrote almost, though not quite, as well as Boswell himself. I have not read, it is true, *Dorando: A Spanish Tale,* which was written during the Douglas case, but I have read Boswell's *Letters* (which are lamentable), and I have read his *Account of Corsica,* which is more lamentable still. It is possible, of course, that the contents of the recently discovered "ebony box" may lead us to revise our estimate of Boswell's character and genius; but I doubt it. I doubt whether we have lost much by the fact that Boswell did not write or publish his threatened biographies of Hume, Sir Robert Sibbald, and Lord Kaimes. For I fear that Boswell on any other subject than Johnson was not quite himself.

This impression is supplemented by considering Dr. Johnson in the works of others. Sir John Hawkins, for instance, was not a man of letters, nor was he endowed with any

<small>Sir John Hawkins.</small>

vivid interest in the personality of others. He was, as we know, "a most unclubbable man." And yet his *Life of Johnson* is eminently readable, and would, were it not for Boswell, be a popular work even today. For through the pages of this dry and stingy attorney pierces the vivid humanity of Johnson, giving to the book a realism and an actuality of which Hawkins was himself probably quite unaware. It could be contended even that Sir John Hawkins gives a more complete and convincing picture of Johnson than does Boswell himself. It is from Hawkins and not from Boswell that we get the picture of the middle period from 1749 to 1756, when Johnson was forming himself as a dictator at the King's Head in Ivy Lane, and founding the earlier group with Dr. Salter, Dr. Hawkesworth, Dr. Dyer, and Mr. Payne. It is from Hawkins that we obtain, even upon the later period, certain sidelights which Boswell failed to observe or understand. It is Hawkins, and not Boswell, who advances the interesting and acute supposition that Johnson was at heart a coward, and that in his later years he was tortured by some specific remorse. There is little in Boswell about the gentler side of Johnson; no picture so illustrative of this aspect as that of Johnson watering his flowers in Bolt Court. Hawkins, again, is far more intelligent and pene-

THE BOSWELL FORMULA

trating on the subject of Johnson's strange seraglio; on his dread of returning home at night to find Mrs. Williams sitting up for him with some grievance against Francis Barber, or Mrs. Desmoulins in the passage with her complaints about "the mute, the officious, the humble Mr. Levett." "Hawky," writes Boswell to Temple, "is no doubt very malevolent. Observe how he talks of me, as if quite unknown!" But, had Boswell realised it, he had something more important than mere misprisal to fear from Sir John Hawkins: he had, to no slight extent, to fear comparison.

Then there is Fanny Burney's "sweet naughty Mrs. Thrale," a lady of immense vitality and charm of whom Boswell is palpably jealous, and to whom he is palpably unjust. For Mrs. Thrale's *Anecdotes of Dr. Johnson*, which she published after her marriage to Piozzi, are, to my mind at least, almost as entertaining as those of Boswell himself. She does not, it is true, convince us that she is producing Johnson's actual words; the lapidary phrase is a little softened and the edges blurred. But what she charmingly calls "her candlelight picture" leaves upon the mind an impression almost as vivid as Boswell's, almost as distinct, and at moments more sympathetic. She brings out the essential childishness of Johnson's character: his

<small>Mrs. Thrale.</small>

petty peevishness on the one hand, his love, on the other, of sheer nonsense and his sense of fun. Boswell does not understand this aspect of his hero. If he refers to it, he refers to it with startled bewilderment, as when Johnson got the giggles at Temple Bar. I do not think, therefore, that one can rightly estimate Boswell until one has read Hawkins, and even the moonstruck Fanny Burney, and above all Mrs. Thrale. Several people could write an entertaining book about Johnson. Boswell could not write "entertainingly" about anything else. This in itself limits his achievement to reasonable proportions.

That it is an achievement, and a very remarkable achievement, it would be unintelligent to deny. His actual achievement. The effect of Boswell's book is permanent and powerful; but two-thirds of this effect are due to "accidental" circumstances, such as charm and opportunity, which have but little to do with "value," and by which Boswell's actual contribution to biography as a branch of creative literature cannot rightly be appraised. Having for the moment, and for the sole purpose of scientific examination, rid our minds of Boswell's charm and discounted his opportunity, let us now attack the remaining third, the actual literary and biographical value of the *Journal* and the *Life of Johnson*.

THE BOSWELL FORMULA

I would wish in the first place to examine the actual quality of Boswell's mind. That Boswell was occasionally silly there can be no doubt. His own comments and allusions are often either commonplace or fatuous. "Nature," he writes at one moment, "seems to have implanted gratitude in all living creatures. The lion mentioned by Aulus Gellius had it." "Each of them," he writes again, "having a black servant was another point of similarity between Johnson and Monboddo." Such false associations could be cited without number, but it is unnecessary to push the point further. That Boswell was frequently an ass is generally admitted. What I want to get at is, was he also a fool? I do not think that he was a fool, nor do I think that he was a genius; but biography—and this is an important point—does not require genius; it requires only a peculiar form of talent. Boswell possessed such a talent. The muscles of his mind were often lax, but he possessed great mental vivacity, he possessed a remarkably independent intellect; he was above all passionately interested in life. Such convictions as he possessed were merely superficial; the essential Boswell was restrained by no inherited habits of thought; his mind was not only inquiring but also open. "You and I," said Johnson, "do not

Quality of Boswell's intelligence.

talk from books." In this generous liberality of mind Boswell, to some extent, was in advance of Johnson; he was certainly in advance of his age. Those of his contemporaries who did not dismiss him as merely disreputable and silly thought him mad. "He is so extraordinary a man," said Queen Charlotte in 1785, "that perhaps he will devise something extraordinary." Even in the *Account of Corsica* Boswell had spoken of his "antipathy to established rules." The temperamental unconventionality thus disclosed developed, at its worst, into mere bumptiousness and bad behaviour; but at its best it was profoundly original and profoundly courageous.

His courage and his originality are the essential qualities of Boswell, and will be examined later.

His literary gifts. I would wish first to draw attention to his actual literary gifts, to those secondary qualities which rendered him so supreme a biographer. His assiduity in writing down Johnson's conversation is, of course, commendable; but stenography is not in itself one of the Muses, nor does mere annotation raise biography to the level of creative art. One looks for construction, for selection, for literary tact; one demands observation, understanding, and a certain excellence of style. How far does Boswell meet these requirements?

THE BOSWELL FORMULA

His style, in the first place, is flowing and pleasant. "I surely have," he wrote to Temple, "the art of writing agreeably." No one could deny the justice of this claim. He possessed a most retentive memory, both visual and oral, and a taste for vivid circumstantial detail. His talent for dramatisation is unquestioned: his description, for instance, of the dinner-party at which a reconciliation was effected between Johnson and Wilkes is as vivid and convincing as could be desired. His psychological gifts, though not very penetrating, are alert. His powers of observation, moreover, are amazing: at moments they attain an almost Proustian delicacy. Take this, for instance, from the *Journal:*

> A gentleman . . . after dinner, was desired by the Duke to go to another room for a specimen of curious marble which His Grace wished to show us. He brought a wrong piece, upon which the Duke sent him back again. He could not refuse: but to avoid any appearance of servility, he whistled as he walked out of the room to show his independency.[1]

Assuredly Boswell was in advance of his age.

The construction of the *Life of Johnson* may, at first sight, appear artless; yet great art was required to fuse into some coherent and readable whole the disordered mass of notes and letters which Boswell had accumulated. The *Journal of a Tour to the*

[1] *Journal of a Tour to the Hebrides*, Everyman edition, p. 350.

Hebrides fell almost naturally into shape, since its outlines and internal divisions were dictated by the duration and stages of the journey itself. In composing the *Life,* however, Boswell was from the outset faced with the problem whether he should write a formal biography like that of Hawkins, or mere *Johnsoniana* like the anecdotes of Mrs. Thrale. He decided to combine the advantages of both methods. The fact that this decision did not utterly destroy the unity of his book proves that Boswell possessed a very remarkable talent for construction and great literary tact. Consider the technical difficulties. Boswell set out to paint on the large canvas of a full-length biography the "Flemish picture" which he desired to compose. It must be remembered that of the seventy-five years of Johnson's life Boswell had direct knowledge of only twenty-one, and that during these twenty-one years he was only in Johnson's company on two hundred and seventy-six days. He thus possessed but shadowy and indirect knowledge of two-thirds of Johnson's life, whereas his material for the remaining third was, although only in patches, embarrassingly detailed. He endeavoured to conceal this discrepancy by the introduction of letters and the blurring of dates. The skill with which the indirect method of the earlier portrait is dovetailed into

THE BOSWELL FORMULA

the direct and vivid manner of the later period is indeed remarkable. We scarcely realise, when reading the book, that out of a rough total of 1250 pages, 1000 are devoted to Johnson after he had met Boswell, and only 250 to the pre-Boswell period. The book, moreover, is written without prescribed divisions or chapters, and yet its interest, its unity of impression, its sheer limpid continuity is sustained throughout. For the *Life of Johnson* is a work of art, not merely in its actual excellence of outline, but in the careful adjustment of internal spaces. We have thus the absence of comment, or rather the very skilful interspacing of comment—the way in which Boswell first provides the evidence, and then, at a later period, confirms by comment the conclusion which the reader had already reached. I would refer you, as a particular instance of this method, to his treatment of Johnson's strange gullibility on all supernatural matters, and his obstinate scepticism in all natural matters. Boswell tells without comment a story of Johnson's belief in ghosts; a few pages later he tells, equally without comment, of his scepticism regarding some quite natural novelty such as stenography; it is not till much later that he comments directly on his strange conjunction of scepticism and gullibility; and by then the reader can recollect and recognise the evidence on which this comment is based. Equally skilful is his manipulation of the elements of surprise and recognition, of expectation and satisfaction. He keeps his reader constantly in mind, and as constantly pays subtle compliments to his memory and his intelligence. He throws out something, such as the story of Johnson and the orange-peel, which he slyly knows will excite curiosity; he then drops the subject; and then, slyly, he returns to it several pages later, knowing well that greater pleasure will be caused if curiosity is not immediately allayed. This is something more than mere adroitness; it is constructive talent of the highest order. Consider also his sense of values; the skill with which he records the conversation of other people to the exact degree necessary to explain and illustrate the remarks of Dr. Johnson; the tact with which, while conveying an intimate picture of himself, he does not obtrude unnecessarily; and how, in the serious passages on Johnson's last illness, he withdraws with unexpected delicacy from the scene. Consider also his very exquisite handling of cumulative detail; the mastery with which the portrait of Johnson is conveyed by an accumulation of slight successive touches until the whole rolling, snorting, rumbling bulk of the man becomes visible, and we feel that he has grown in intimacy as the book proceeds;

that we have become aware, quite naturally, of his brown stockings, his disordered buttons, the dust settling in his wig as he bangs two folios together, the way he cut his nails, of his servants, his teapot, and his cat. And this rapid method of portrayal was certainly deliberate. "It appears to me," he wrote to Bishop Percy, "that mine is the best plan of biography that can be conceived; for my readers will as near as may be accompany Johnson in his progress, and, as it were, see each scene as it happened." It is indeed amazing that Boswell should have succeeded so triumphantly. He was, during the whole period when he was writing the book, distracted by ill-health, by prolonged dissipation, and by acute financial and domestic troubles. It is true that he was assisted by Malone, but the latter was engaged at the time with his own edition of Shakespeare, and can in no sense be considered as more than a discerning proof-reader. The credit of Boswell's *Johnson* belongs to Boswell alone. His work was a deliberate and highly successful innovation in the art of biography. In what exactly did this innovation consist?

The several elements which compose Boswell's
Boswell's method had all been attempted before.
originality. It was Johnson himself who had invented and perfected the method of truthful por-

traiture and of the realistic biography. The device of introducing original letters and documents was as old as Eadmer, and had been exploited by Mason. The device of introducing anecdote and actual conversations had been brought to a high pitch of perfection in the French *ana*, had been employed in the *Table Talk of Selden*, and had been admirably applied to Pope and his circle by Spence. Boswell's originality was not that he invented any of these mechanical aids to biography, but that he combined them in a single whole. That, as least, had never been done before. Nor was this his innovation due to any accident; it was perfectly self-conscious and deliberate. What he calls "the peculiar plan of this biographical undertaking" had remained in his mind for over twenty-five years. He experimented with it, not very successfully, in his early Corsican journal; he gave it a trial in his *Journal of a Tour to the Hebrides*, which he published in 1785. Much of the latter had been read by Johnson himself, and Boswell had profited by his criticism, as he profited by the subsequent criticisms of the public. The notes which he accumulated during the twenty-one years of his acquaintance with Johnson were continually being sifted and remodelled. He perfected his method. "I found," he writes, "from experience that to collect my friend's conversation so as to

THE BOSWELL FORMULA

exhibit it with any degree of its original flavour, it was necessary to write it down without delay. To record his sayings after some distance of time was like preserving or pickling long-kept and faded fruits or other vegetables, which, when in that state, have little or nothing of their taste when fresh."[1]

But it was not merely that Boswell perfected the annotative and the analytical methods of biography. His great achievement is that he combined them with the synthetic. He was able, by sheer constructive force, to project his detached photographs with such continuity and speed that the effect produced is that of motion and of life. It is this that I mean by "the Boswell formula"—a formula which, in the present generation, aided by our familiarity with the cinematograph, might well be still further developed.

His courage. Boswell's claim to be the greatest of English biographers is thus justified not merely by the entertainment which his work provides, but by the fact that it represents a deliberate and extremely difficult combination of methods, that he invented a highly original and fruitful formula. I would wish before finishing this lecture to do justice to Boswell's courage in persisting in

[1] Boswell's *Life of Johnson*, Everyman edition, vol. ii, p. 134.

his own method. For people were already becoming alarmed at the growing public taste for truth. They were alarmed by Curll's ventures, they were seriously alarmed by Spence. Peter Pindar's *Bozzy and Piozzi; or The British Biographers,* dates from 1786, and in the following year Canning attacked Boswell's method in the *Microcosm.* Dr. Waldo Dunn, to whose work on English biography I have been frequently indebted, has unearthed an even more specific attack which dates from 1788. "Biography," wrote a certain Mr. Vicesimus Knox, "is every day descending from its dignity. Instead of an instructive recital, it is becoming an instrument to the mere gratification of an impertinent, not to say malignant, curiosity. . . . I am apprehensive that the custom of exposing the nakedness of eminent men of every type will have an unfavorable influence on virtue. It may teach men to fear celebrity." These attacks, it must be realised, were delivered at a moment when Boswell, although ill and tried by domestic trouble, was composing his masterpiece. And Boswell persisted.

V

THE NINETEENTH CENTURY

Boswell's formula essentially English—Nineteenth-century earnestness—Pre-Victorian biography—Thomas Moore—Southey—Minor biographies before 1840—Macaulay—Lockhart—His constructive genius—His dramatic instinct—His power of selection—His contribution to the biographical method—Victorian biography—Froude's *Carlyle*.

IN the formula invented and perfected by James Boswell our national talent for biography found its full expression. The gay realism of Chaucer, the sly yet irreverent analysis of Aubrey, the dramatic gifts of Roger North, the synthetic talent of Walton—all these combined in Boswell to create a method of biography which is essentially national and essentially suited to the British temperament. Consider, for instance, how few Frenchmen can appreciate Boswell; how Taine muddled his whole Johnson section; how ill-at-ease the Latin mind becomes when confronted with the Boswell formula, not knowing whether to laugh *at* or *with*, confused by the absence of any apparent purpose or design. For the Anglo-

Boswell's formula essentially English.

Saxon mind is at its best when proceeding inductively, building up the facts of life slowly, humourously, patiently; interpreting these jumbled facts not by any consecutive process of reason, but by the sweeping lighthouse flashes of intuition and imagination. This, our national habit of guess-work, while it creates "actuality," has its disadvantages; but at least it is our own; and when we depart from it and endeavour to copy our Latin neighbours, endeavour to be clear and earnest and logical—at such moments our happy April humour is taken from us, and the English genius, through a mist of sobriety, shines as a pompous winter sun.

Something like this happened to nineteenth-century biography. It all began splendidly. We had Moore and Southey and Lockhart; but then came earnestness, and with earnestness hagiography descended on us with its sullen cloud, and the Victorian biographer scribbled laboriously by the light of shaded lamps. It cannot be sufficiently emphasised that the art of biography is intellectual and not emotional. So long as the intellect is undisturbed by emotion you have good biography. The moment, however, that any emotion (such as reverence, affection, ethical desires, religious belief) intrudes upon the composition of a biography, that biography is doomed.

Nineteenth-century earnestness

THE NINETEENTH CENTURY

Of all such emotions religious earnestness is the most fatal to pure biography. Not only does it carry with it all the vices of hagiography (the desire to prove a case, to depict an example—the sheer perversion, for such purposes, of fact), but it disinterests the biographer in his subject. A deep belief in a personal deity destroys all deep belief in the unconquerable personality of man. Nor is this all. Religious earnestness tempts people to think in terms of dualism; to draw, that is, a sharp line between the material and the spiritual, between the body and the soul, between the mortal and what they would call the immortal. This sort of thing is very bad for biography. There is no such dualism in man; there is personality, and that is all; and if one thinks of personality in terms of dualism one is, in fact, not thinking of personality at all. It is this religious earnestness which is responsible for the catastrophic failure of Victorian biography. Just as in the seventeenth century the early current of pure biography was checked by metaphysical preoccupations, so was the full and sparkling stream of our riper tradition rendered fat and sluggish by the evangelicalism of the Victorians.

It did not begin at once. The Boswell tradition was still potent till 1840. At the outset of the century critical opinion was still absolutely sound regarding the ethics of biography. I quote the following from the *Edinburgh Review* of April 1803:—

> When a man has moved through life with nothing but innocence or common virtue to recommend him, we would rather subscribe to the marble-cutter and the author of a monumental narrative, than read the biographies of his friends and admirers. . . . The deeds which lie in common fame must, in a biographical sketch, be fixed down to some real person, not to an abstract being. . . . Unless the biographer will condescend to lower his attention, his work will neither be useful, nor satisfactory, nor pleasing, nor, in a word, biographical. . . . That truth which relations dare not hear, it is criminal to conceal from the world. For these reasons we consider it to be highly improper, to say the least of it, that much deference should ever be paid to the feelings of relations: in these cases they are the parties least concerned.

How came it that this eminently intelligent appreciation of the functions of biography was so rapidly obscured? We sometimes fail to realise the vast gulf which yawned between the men born before the French Revolution and those born, say, in 1795. Let me take a striking instance. A gap of not more than seven years separates the birth-year of Byron from that of Thomas Arnold. And yet, on 1st February 1819, at a moment when Arnold was wrestling with scruples about "that most awful subject—the doctrine of the blessed Trinity" ("Do not start, my dear Coleridge"), Byron at Venice was writing:

> Let not a monument give you or me hopes
> Since not a pinch of dust is left to Cheops.

Both Byron and Arnold, in their respective manners, were extreme; and yet the vast majority of Englishmen born in 1785 would have been bewildered by Arnold's earnestness, and the vast majority of Englishmen born in 1795 would have been horrified by the flippancy of Byron. For within that short decade the germ of seriousness had infected the youth of England. The malady spread with amazing rapidity; the older generation went down like ninepins. And on 30th August 1828 Thomas Arnold arrived at Rugby. On that day Victorianism was born.

The religious earnestness of the Arnold generation, as being inimical to pure biography, was inimical to the Boswell formula. It was some years, however, before the true Victorian fog descended upon English biography. The complete rejection of truthful representation, the bag-and-baggage return to hagiography, cannot be dated earlier than 1844, the year in which Stanley published his egregious *Life of Arnold*. Between 1800 and 1840 several excellent biographies, and one at least of supreme merit, were composed in the

Pre-Victorian biography.

best Boswell tradition. We have Thomas Moore's *Life of Sheridan* (1815), and his more famous *Letters and Journals of Lord Byron*, which was published in 1830. The latter work has not, I think, been accorded the praise that it deserves. Within the limit of his regard for Byron's executors and relations, Moore did essay, if not to tell the truth, then at least to avoid untruth; and in this endeavour he was skilful, courageous, and persistent. The book is vivid and agreeable, and went far to destroy the wholly false impression of Byron which had been founded on his earlier poems. Moore, as a biographer, is quite in the good tradition. Had he been a brave man he could have produced the most arresting of all biographies. But he was not a brave man, and his work, though something more than merely competent, must always when compared to his opportunity, remain a disappointment.

Thomas Moore.

If Moore represents the Boswell tradition, somewhat diluted by the milk of caution, Southey recall Walton, in that the synthetic element with him is more stressed than the analytical. His *Life of Nelson* (1813) and his *Life of Wesley* (1820) have been extensively praised and are to this day popular and admired. Southey's powers of selection and arrangement are indeed

Southey.

THE NINETEENTH CENTURY

admirable; his style is fluent and at moments picturesque; his dramatic sense, as in the famous description of the battle of Trafalgar, never interferes with his somewhat rigid conception of literary proportion. His biographies are unquestionably works of art, but they lack that sense of movement, of internal development, which can alone awake the full zest of personal interest. There are moments when one's respect for Southey's gifts produces a glow of admiration; but the glow is somewhat tepid, nor is the effect very lasting. One can be warmed by Southey, but one can scarcely be fired; for Southey, in the last resort, is not alive. The germ of seriousness has already attacked his brain.

Moore, Southey, and Lockhart are the three outstanding figures in what might be called the pre-Victorian period, and it is Lockhart who produced the second greatest biography which we possess.

Minor biographies before 1840.

Before, however, I discuss the *Life of Scott* I would wish to mention certain minor works which are interesting as secondary landmarks in the progress of the biographical art. William Godwin's *Life of Chaucer* (1803) has been dubbed by Professor Lounsbury as "the most worthless piece of biography in the English language," but it is interesting as being one of the first of those "reconstruc-

115

tional biographies" to which the nineteenth century devoted so much labour and scholarship. Another such biography is Scott's *Life of Dryden* (1808), in which the literary atmosphere of the age of Dryden is dealt with in a scientific spirit. Each poem or play is examined and criticised in relation to its context or times, and there is a long and instructive review of the state of literature when Dryden arrived. Such books are the true precursors of the "life-and-times" method of biography—a method which, aided by the scientific spirit of nineteenth-century history, is responsible for the monumental industry of works like David Masson's *Life of Milton* and *Drummond of Hawthornden* (1859-80), Spedding's *Bacon* (1861), and Aitken's *Steele* (1889). Less scholarly, but far more entertaining than these, is Monk's *Bentley* (1833), a work in which, after frankly recognising that "great learning is not always accompanied by the graces of personal character," Mr. Monk proceeds, with the aid of documents, to disclose the marked deficiencies of Bentley's temperament, his avarice, his litigiousness, his arrogance, his actual dishonesty. The work is frank, convincing, and urbane. It is by no means the least among the pre-Victorian biographies.

Of great importance to the development of biography were the twenty-seven biographical and critical essays which Macaulay contributed to the *Edinburgh Review* between August 1825 and October 1844. These essays, in form at least, were reviews of other people's biographies, and Macaulay did not claim to be a direct biographer himself. Yet his astounding powers of condensation, his rhetorical fluency, his graphic gifts, his apparent truth and conviction, familiarised the great English public with the biographical essay in its most readable and attractive form. Macaulay, more than any writer before Froude, taught the Victorian public that biography need not necessarily be dull. His influence, on the whole, was salutary. We may question, however, whether his predilection for dramatic "types," his superficiality, his lack of real psychological insight, and his unconquerable personal and party bias would have enabled him to write an extended biography of any deep or permanent value. He was an excellent and highly useful critic of biography. I doubt whether he would have proved a really great biographer.

Macaulay.

Lockhart, on the other hand, is the second greatest (I am sometimes inclined to think the greatest) of all British biographers. His *Life of Scott* (1836-38) is, after

Lockhart's "Scott."

Boswell's *Johnson*, the most convincing biography we possess. "I have endeavoured," he states, "to lay before the reader those parts of Sir Walter's character to which we have access, as they were indicated in his sayings and doings through the long series of his years—making use, whenever it was possible, of his own letters and diaries rather than of any other materials—but refrained from obtruding almost anything of comment. It was my wish to let the character develop itself."[1] Lockhart's purpose and method were thus deliberate. His success in executing that purpose is beyond praise. The book is long, but the inductive or cumulative method necessitates length; and in this case the method is abundantly justified by the interest which the book arouses and the conviction which it leaves behind. Lockhart has also been criticised, and notably by Carlyle, for his lack of construction, for his failure fully to digest and sift the vast material with which he has to deal. It is a fact that Lockhart almost succumbed under the mass of Sir Walter's muniments, but I cannot see myself that the book, as completed, reflects this physical exhaustion, nor can I myself observe that "lack of spontaneity" of which others have complained. The work, it is true, proceeds somewhat leisurely; but

[1] Lockhart's *Life of Scott*, vol. vii, p. 398.

THE NINETEENTH CENTURY

this in itself reflects the happy uniformity of Scott's existence. The detail, it is again true, is often trivial; but it is by the massing of such detail that Lockhart, in the exact manner of Balzac, achieves his effect. Carlyle, who admired the book sincerely, regretted that it was a "compilation" rather than a "composition." This criticism is difficult to understand. No work, if one examines the machinery, shows more careful "composition" than Lockhart's *Life of Scott*. With what skill, for instance, does he avoid a break of continuity when passing from the earlier Scott to the Scott of his own recollection! How perfectly, in other words, does he fuse the indirect with the direct narration! We have no sudden sense of Lockhart's own appearance on the scene. What Andrew Lang has called his "total lack of self-consciousness" enables him to enter his own narrative unobserved: he merely slips into the room, the conversation continues; it is only insensibly that we realise that it has all become more convincing and more real. With what skill again, with what rare insight, does he refrain from any formal discourse on Scott's literary development, allowing us gradually to realise this development through its proper atmosphere—in the atmosphere, that is, of hilarious walking tours in the Border country, or through the peat-smoke of some

[margin: Lockhart's constructive genius.]

wayside hut! We have a hint, at first, of Percy's *Reliques*; we have a paragraph or two on the Germans and *Goetz von Berlichingen*; but those were books, and could be treated in the study. Scott's own essential genius, however, is disclosed to us incidentally, and, as is fitting, in the open air. There is little comment; there is little literary criticism or appreciation; and yet Lockhart's mastery of treatment and of composition conveys all the elucidation that is required. I do not know myself of any better instances of consummate literary tact. Scarcely less striking is Lockhart's cumulative method in disclosing Scott's character and charm. The whole thing is done in a succession of innumerable small touches, which are at intervals summarised and co-ordinated by the introduction of some external observer—of Washington Irving, of Thomas Moore, or of some less distinguished witness, such as Mr. Morritt. "Well, Miss Sophia," James Ballantyne asks one of the Scott children, "how do you like the *Lady of the Lake?*" "Oh, I have not read it," she answers. "Papa says there's nothing so bad for young people as reading bad poetry." It is by slight touches such as this that the irresistible charm of Scott is cumulatively conveyed.

A further, and to me equally incredible, criticism

of Lockhart is that, unlike Boswell and Froude, he does not possess the dramatic instinct. Such a criticism is simply unintelligent. What could be more essentially dramatic than the treatment of his minor characters—of Erskine, of Laidlaw, and of Tom Purdie? What, again, could be more dramatic than the celebrated description of Crabbe's visit, or than the vivid picture of William Menzies' dinner-party on that night in June 1814? The hot room; the younger men go to the library; it has a north window; the window looks obliquely upon Castle Street, and thus upon another lighted window through which a hand, and only a hand, can be seen writing, writing, pausing only to place another finished sheet upon the pile. Some one suggests that it is an attorney's clerk finishing his evening work: "No, boys," the host exclaims; "I well know what hand it is—'tis Walter Scott's." "This," comments Lockhart, "was the hand that, in the evenings of three summer weeks, wrote the two last volumes of *Waverley*." The whole passage arrests attention and leaves a lasting impression, and Lockhart was perfectly aware, when he wrote it, that future critics would spot the passage and write of it with all the enthusiasm which it deserves. For Lockhart, with all his "total lack of self-consciousness," was a highly conscious artist.

Take again his power of selection; the actual mastery with which he secures his effect at the exact moment desired; his extreme sensitiveness to what is passing in his reader's mind. Scott's passion for dogs, for instance, was doubtless admirable and charming, but in clumsier hands the trait might have been exaggerated and have become tiresome. Lockhart, however, manages the canine-friend business with delicate discretion. He alludes to it at intervals; the reader insensibly adds a dog or two to his mental picture of Sir Walter; but it is only at the end, it is only when Scott, at Naples, enters into the final decline, that the thing is put into its exact proportion. It is then, and in an atmosphere of gathering dissolution, that the dogs are brought into the foreground. The bemused mind of the semi-paralytic is allowed to dwell on them; they become symbols; they achieve a seriousness which, while perfectly accurate, does not jar the sense, as it would have jarred if stressed in the earlier portions of the biography. Take also the skill with which Lockhart places his anecdotes. There is a story about Scott not noticing, on returning to Abbotsford, that his wife had arrayed the furniture in a bright new chintz. Mrs. Scott was hurt at his failure to observe this innovation; in the end she could stand it no

THE NINETEENTH CENTURY

longer, and drew his attention to it; he was all contrition, he was all admiration. The anecdote is slight in itself, but it is timed at exactly the right moment; it is timed at the moment when the reader is a little disgusted by Scott's delight at the flattering reception accorded to him by all those important people whom he had met in Paris in July 1815. The little world of the Abbotsford parlour is given greater prominence than the big world of the Emperor Alexander, the Prince of Orange, Lord Cathcart, the Hetman of the Cossacks. The reader had begun to feel uneasy; he is at once reassured by the story about the chintz at Abbotsford. It is with similar delicacy that Lockhart approaches the subject of Scott's perfectly healthy snobbishness. His stern sense of duty obliged him to reveal this somewhat grotesque aspect of his father-in-law's character. But he prepared the reader in advance. The passage, the inevitable passage, is prefaced by a few anecdotes indicative of Scott's contempt for those who looked down upon their social or intellectual inferiors, his objection to the use of the words "common" or "vulgar." The reader, thus prepared, is readily able to swallow the fact that Scott, while deprecating all tendency to look down on inferiors, was himself unduly inclined to look up to those whom he regarded as his superiors. The truth is told; the pill is swallowed; and the reader takes it gently with the jam which that great artificer had introduced.

I have said enough to show why Lockhart should be considered as second only to Boswell in the art of biography. He adopted Boswell's method in the sense that he worked up his portrait on the impressionist method. He was wise enough to avoid the annotative system and to eschew all stenographic records of conversation. Such a method would, with Walter Scott, have failed most dismally; for Scott was no conversationalist; Scott had to be painted out of doors. And it was in this way, with all sympathy and all understanding, with consummate art, with absolute frankness, that Lockhart painted him.

Lockhart's contribution to the biographical method.

His biography was hotly attacked. He was accused (for we are by now in 1838) of being unkind and disloyal, of revealing faults that should have been buried in the grave, of not allowing Scott to live for posterity in his works alone. Carlyle, I am glad to say, defended him. "For our part," he wrote, "we hope that all manner of biographies that are written in England will henceforth be written so. If it is fit that they be written otherwise, then it is still fitter that they be not written at all: to

THE NINETEENTH CENTURY

produce, not things, but ghosts of things can never be the duty of man." "How delicate," he wrote again, "how decent is English biography, bless its mealy mouth! A Damocles Sword of Respectability hangs forever over the poor English life-writer ... and reduces him to the verge of paralysis."

By the year 1840 the tide of Victorian biography was already setting in. The younger generation, the earnest generation of Arnold, had come to man's estate; the older generation (who had been a little dismayed by such books as Medwin's *Conversations of Lord Byron*, or by that scandalous volume, *Contemporary Portraits*, which Colburn published in 1824) capitulated without a murmur. The Boswell tradition was dead: people reverted with relief to the old, unworthy origins of English biography. It is not, I think, necessary to trace in any detail the developments of English biography between 1838 and 1882, between the date of Lockhart's *Scott* and that of Froude's *Carlyle*. The number of biographies published during this period is enormous, but, in so far as they are "impure" biographies, they have little direct bearing on the evolution of the pure biographic strain. Hagiography, as I have already said, returned in stately triumph with Dean Stanley's *Life of Arnold* in 1844, and continued throughout the

<small>Victorian biography.</small>

century, culminating in such works as Mr. Horton's study of Tennyson in the "Saintly Lives" series of Messrs. Dent (1900). The elegiac or commemorative strain was responsible for innumerable widow or family biographies, of which the best is Mrs. Grote's charming study of her husband (1873), of which the average types are Mrs. Kingsley's biography dedicated "to the beloved memory of a righteous man" (1877) or Mr. Cross's *Life of George Eliot* (1884), and of which the worst, so far as I know, is Lady Burton's two-volume oration on her curious husband. Such works need not detain us, since they will survive only as literary curiosities, or at best as works of reference. The damage which the Victorians did to biography is sufficiently realised. I would wish rather to indicate what were the positive contributions which they made. In the first place, they provided the biographer with a large reading public; in the second place, they perfected the reconstructional biography and produced vast works of erudition, such as Spedding's *Bacon* and David Masson's *Life of Milton;* in the third place, they exploited foreign biography, and gave us such admirable studies as Lewes' *Goethe,* as Carlyle's *Frederick,* as Seeley's *Stein,* as Morley's *Rousseau;* in the fourth place, they invented what I must call "biography for students"—a form of history which under Leslie Stephen developed between 1882 and 1891 into that great work, *The Dictionary of National Biography*, and which in 1877 inspired Morley to edit the scarcely less admirable "English Men of Letters" series; and in the fifth place, they created the professional biographer and the official biography, they produced men like John Forster, they set the standard for such highly competent works as Trevelyan's *Macaulay*, and they popularised the two-volume *Life and Letters* with which we are so familiar. I do not pretend that all this has had any very enduring influence on the evolution of biography as a branch of English literature. I contend only that when the art of biography returned to England it found itself much indebted for its material to the competent and conscientious industry of these Victorians.

I shall now resume my study of biography proper, which was revived by Froude between 1882 and 1884. I shall be blamed, doubtless, for omitting Carlyle's *Sterling* (1851) and Mrs. Gaskell's *Charlotte Brontë* (1857). I do not, however, regard these two books as being in the direct succession. John Sterling, as all inheritors of unfulfilled renown, was an interesting psychological problem. Carlyle in his highly idyllic book does not solve that problem. He indicates, it is true, that

<small>Froude's "Carlyle."</small>

Sterling was as brilliant and as ineffective as summer lightning, but he does not explain Sterling; he merely explains how right, always, is Thomas Carlyle, and how wrong, always, was Archdeacon Hare. Mrs. Gaskell, for her part, made a brilliant endeavour to depict Miss Brontë, even with "the slight astringencies of her character," as she was. The book is an excellent sentimental novel replete with local colour; but it is not a biography, since one of the central conceptions, that of Branwell Brontë's intrigue with a married woman, is sheer inexcusable fiction. It deals with the life of an individual, and it is certainly composed with high literary skill; but it does not fulfil the third requirement of pure biography; it is not, and in a very essential respect, accurate; it is a story, but it is not history. With Froude, however, we return to biography in its purest form. Froude was not an earnest-minded man: as an historian he reacted against the scientific method in favour of the picturesque; as a biographer he reacted against the commemorative method in favour of truth. He did not care for hagiography. As a young man, it is true, he contributed a life of St. Neot to Newman's *Lives of the Saints*, but when the book was published he described the whole business as "nonsense," and consoled himself by writing an improper novel under the pseudonym of "Zeta," and by publishing, a few months later, his *Nemesis of Faith*. On the death of Carlyle he found himself the sole surviving executor; he found himself in a stronger position even than Boswell. He profited by this position; he carried out exactly the rules which Carlyle in his review of Lockhart's *Scott* has himself laid down. Between 1881 and 1884 he published nine fat volumes, which, while fully disclosing the dogged genius, the rugged intellectual honesty of Carlyle, also disclosed his egoism, his conceit, his Calvinistic cruelty, his surly obtuseness to all interests other than his own. Carlyle in a letter to Sterling once described himself as a "poor concrete reality, very offensive now and then." It is this reality which Froude has portrayed. He was not an accurate writer, and there are passages in which the "momentary ardour of his imagination" leads him astray. But his inaccuracy, unlike the inaccuracy of Mrs. Gaskell, is not essential, and the final impression left by his work is one of absolute and convincing actuality. Froude had to choose between the alternative of giving a truthful and as such a disagreeable representation of Carlyle, and that of writing no biography at all. He chose the former alternative, and a yell of dismay arose from the Victorians. The polemics that ensued reverberated like thunder: Tennyson, down at Aldworth, boomed his disapprobation; the smoking-room of the

Athenæum seethed with elderly, outraged indignation; and Mrs. Oliphant, more in sorrow than in anger, wrote a long article on the ethics of biography in the *Contemporary Review*. Froude, it was universally admitted, had shown execrable taste: he was a Judas, he was a traitor, he was a ghoul. The word caught on. Where, they asked, was this ghoulish method of biography tending, where would it end? It desecrated, they said, the sanctities of private life; it revealed, they said, secrets which should remain for ever hidden in the grave; it was disturbing, it was unpleasant, nay, more, it was positively heartless. Amid all this dust and shouting there was one point, however, that escaped attention; they did not notice that Froude had introduced a new element into the art of English biography—a dangerous and perhaps pernicious element which had not occurred to Boswell, which is wholly absent from the *Life of Scott*. On p. 348 of the second volume of Froude's biography there is a description of how Carlyle, at the age of thirty-eight, subjected himself to a severe cross-examination in his journal. "One discovery," says Froude, "came to him as a startling surprise." The journal is then quoted. "On the whole art thou not among the *vainest* of living men? At bottom among the very *vainest*? Oh, the sorry, mad ambitions that lurk in thee.

. . ." And so on, in Carlyle's best Irvingite manner, Froude quotes the whole passage. He makes no further comment; he leaves the reader with that one introductory sentence about the "startling surprise."

For Froude was the first to introduce into English biography the element of satire.

VI

THE PRESENT AGE

Review of previous lectures—The historical method—The evolution of English biography—The differentiation of biography—Twentieth-century biography—Sir Edmund Gosse—*Father and Son* (1907)—Mr. Lytton Strachey—*Queen Victoria* (1921)—The future of biography—The end of "pure" biography.

I HAVE now traced the development of English biography from its rudimentary origins in saga and

Review of previous lectures.

elegy to the satirical form of biography tentatively practised by Froude. I have throughout adopted the convention of speaking (as if I really believed in such things) of "influences" and "innovators," of "reactionaries" and of "pioneers." I have told you of Bede and Asser, of Eadmer and William of Malmesbury. I have attributed to these people conscious artistic or biographical purposes which, I well know, they did not possess. I have contended that Roper "introduced" vivid dialogue, that Cavendish "introduced" deliberate inductive composition. I have examined the "influence" of Plutarch and Tacitus, the "influence" of the French character-sketch. I have given you Lord Herbert, Lady Fanshawe, Mrs. Hutchinson, and the Duchess of Newcastle, and have constrained each of these people to "contribute" something definite to my story, to notch a mark upon my measure. I have derided Sprat as a "reactionary" and have eulogised Aubrey as a "pioneer." Walton, being an ethical biographer, had to be explained away. Dryden also was somewhat vague; but with Roger North I was again able to speak convincingly of "pure" biography, and to represent him as in the direct succession between Aubrey and Boswell. Johnson and Mason were extremely helpful, since they not only formulated their own theories of biography, but they formulated them in such a manner as to accord with my own. Boswell, for his part, was an obvious landing: we paused to take breath. It was easy to dwell for a moment on Boswell, since he, at least, composed his biography on certain self-conscious principles, and after careful study of his own "influences" and "predecessors." From Boswell to Lockhart was an easy step; nor could one go very wrong in attributing to moral and religious earnestness the blight that ensued. Stanley's *Arnold* undoubtedly marks a date. So also does Froude's *Carlyle*. But do not for one moment imagine that I believe that any of these people (with the possible exception of Boswell) were conscious of what they were doing, were aware of the "tendencies" which they represented or of the "influences" to which they had succumbed. The development of the human intellect from generation to generation can rarely be ascribed to recognisable causes; it must generally be ascribed to that intricate weaving and unweaving of taste and distaste, that kaleidoscopic and continuous reshaping of intellect and indifference, of surprise and expectation, which we call, somewhat indolently, "the spirit of the age." A given individual's attitude towards life and literature is moulded far more by the things he dislikes than by the things he likes, by his rejections rather than by his acceptances. Even those literary "influences" which actually go to form a writer are generally "influences" which he himself would scarcely recognise, or remember, or admit. They come to him when his mind is still in process of crystallisation, and in forms which, when once his mind has crystallised, he would often repudiate.

Subject to this qualification, the historical method has its value. It is, in the first place, a convenient convention. It is much less cumbrous, for instance, to speak of Froude as having "introduced" into biography the spirit of satire, than to say that the peculiar brand of sceptical detachment which we realise to be the main element

The historical method.

in twentieth-century biography can first be recognised, although only in germinal form, in Froude's treatment of the Carlyles. In the second place, the historical method, although it often falsifies essential proportions, does in the end convey an impression of growth, does in fact indicate a line of development. Let me now look back and summarise that development as expressed in the slow and somewhat confused evolution of English biography.

I shall approach this summary from the point of view not of the writer but of the reader. No branch of literature has been more sensitive than biography to the "spirit of the age"; over no form of literary composition have the requirements of the reading public exercised so marked and immediate an influence. The development of biography is primarily the development of the taste for biography. It is from this aspect that I wish to review the matter. Biography was invented to satisfy the commemorative instinct: the family wished to commemorate the dead, and we had elegies, laments, and runic inscriptions; the tribe wished to commemorate its heroes, and we had saga and epic; the Church wished to commemorate its founders, and we had the early lives of the Saints. Biography, thereafter, fell into the hands of the ecclesiastics, who were the

The evolution of English biography.

sole exponents of culture. To the commemorative element they added a didactic element, and the hagiologies were written with a definitely ethical, though sometimes merely a sectarian, purpose. Curiosity, embryonic only in the early chronicles, developed slowly between the eighth and the fourteenth centuries. Bede, Asser, Eadmer, and William of Malmesbury are the landmarks in its development; but until the age of Chaucer this curiosity expressed itself in vague wonderings about the supernatural rather than in any realistic interest in the lives and characters of human beings. The year 1387 is a highly interesting date in the evolution of English biography. In that year Chaucer conceived the idea of his *Canterbury Tales*. Chaucer was a highly original genius, but in embarking on his work he must have had some audience in mind; he must have felt that a certain public, a certain circle of readers, would relish what he was going to say. What was that public? How came it that in 1387 there existed a definite if limited taste for realism, humour, and gentle satire, a taste for what, after all, was analytical psychology? How came it that this taste subsided, that the fourteenth and fifteenth centuries failed to exploit the Chaucerian vein? The fault lies primarily with the bad taste of the Court, who in those days were the sole representatives of the secular reader. It was the Court's subservience to foreign influence that diverted the taste for realism into a taste for romance. This early spring of robust native curiosity was quenched in the sands of unreality; it was not till the sixteenth century that it revived. The books of Roper and Cavendish, though marred by vestiges of their commemorative and didactic heredity, are indications that psychological curiosity—the desire, that is, to learn a man's character rather than his exploits—still existed. In the memoirs of the seventeenth century, above all in Aubrey and the Duchess of Newcastle, this native stream of actuality can still be recognised; but the main current had already been diverted by the drama, and the trickle that survived was trapped by external influences—by pietism, by Puritanism, by metaphysics, by the passion for Plutarch, Theophrastus, and the rest. The eighteenth century was the great age of English biography: we had North and Mason; we had Johnson and Boswell; the same tradition gave us Moore and Lockhart. But in 1840 moral earnestness again intervened, and the art of English biography, until 1881, declined.

What can we deduce from this series of advances and regressions? How can we explain why the interest in biography on reaching a certain stage of development is apt to recede? Why is it that in the fourteenth century we had an impulse towards good biography, and that in the fifteenth century this impulse waned; that in the sixteenth century biography made a signal advance, only to recede again in the century that followed; that in the eighteenth century it reached a high state of excellence, and thereafter collapsed under the Victorians? There is something more in all this than the usual fluctuations of taste, than the natural reaction of one generation against the preferences and pleasures of their predecessors. The causes of this rhythmic ebb and flow are more profound than the accidents and whims which modify most literary fashions. Biography having no claim to be a specific branch of literature was never properly isolated. It possessed no independent existence; it rose and fell simply with the public interest in human personality, with their taste for psychology. This taste, in its turn, is governed by the ebb and flow of religious belief. In periods when the reading public believe in God and in the life after death, their interest centres on what they would call the eternal verities, their interest in mundane verities declines. At such periods biography becomes deductive, ethical, didactic, or merely superficial. In periods, however, of speculation, doubt, or scepticism the reading public become predominantly interested in human behaviour, and biography, in order to meet this interest, becomes inductive, critical, detached, and realistic. If biography possessed a more distinct identity, had it ever been properly differentiated from other species of literary composition, it would doubtless have its own vitality and be less of a straw on the tide of taste. But biography does not, as yet, possess a distinct identity. It is entangled with other interests —with that, for instance, of history, fiction, and science.

The nineteenth-century biographers, for their part, were particularly incapable of evolving any conception of their own function. Some were blinded by the commemorative aspect, and composed elegies, apologies, idylls. Others succumbed to hagiology, and produced not portraits but ethical types. Others, again, were attracted by history, and we had the "life-and-times" method of biography. A few were tempted by fiction, and there were many works published as fanciful as Lady Morgan's *Salvator Rosa*. You will have observed, for instance, that I have made scant reference to Carlyle's *Frederick the Great*, convinced though I be that this magnificent work had an immense "influence" on the Victorian realisation of personality. But the book essentially

The differentiation of biography.

is written on the "life-and-times" method, and as such is less a study of an individual than a study of history expressed in and through an individual. Similarly, I have dismissed Mrs. Gaskell's *Charlotte Brontë*, since, in sacrificing truth to sentimentality, those amiable though misleading volumes fall under the heading of historical fiction. Until the twentieth century no serious endeavour was made to isolate biography, to differentiate it from cognate modes of narration. By applying the tests of individuality on the one hand and on the other hand of truth, we have ourselves succeeded in differentiating biography from both history and fiction. There are few today who would not admit that a work which does not deal primarily with an individual, or which is not truthful, is something other than a biography. But the process of differentiation is even today incomplete. We have as yet not grappled with the relation of biography to science on the one hand and to literature on the other. It is with this problem that I would now wish to deal; for until it has been stated we cannot rightly appreciate modern tendencies, or appraise the important contribution made to twentieth-century biography by Mr. Lytton Strachey and Sir Edmund Gosse.

The present taste for biography proceeds, on the one hand, from the somewhat indolent interest taken by the library public in the more personal side of history, and, on the other, from a really intelligent and cultivated relish for psychology. It is this latter interest which is the more important and which I would wish to examine. For this intelligent interest in biography is in fact a dual interest: it is partly "scientific" and partly "literary." By "scientific" I mean that interest which insists on facts, on those "parallel circumstances and kindred images to which we readily conform our minds." I do not contend that this scientific interest is as yet very general or very profound. It is leading us to insist on nothing but the truth, but it has not as yet led us to insist on all the truth. To that extent it is superficially scientific. The very real pleasure which the intelligent reader today derives from biography, proceeds in general from no very active energy of thought: his responses are stirred by languid processes of identification and comparison. He identifies himself with certain characters in a biography, and he compares his own feelings and experiences with theirs. This process, as Lord Oxford has remarked, is very pleasurable. "It brings comfort, it enlarges sympathy, it expels selfishness, it quickens aspiration." Moreover, this intelligent interest in biography is increasing. The less people believe in theology the

Twentieth-century biography.

more do they believe in human experience. And it is to biography that they go for this experience. On the other hand, the intelligent reader also demands literary form. He asks that the details which are given him should be based on that "certainty of knowledge which not only excludes mistakes but fortifies veracity"; he asks for more and more of these details: and yet he insists that the mass of material be presented in a readable form. This dual demand throws a severe burden on the twentieth-century biographer. To meet the interest in "scientific" biography he has to accumulate a vast amount of authentic material; to meet the concurrent desire for "literary" biography he has to produce this material in synthetic form. A synthesis, however, requires a thesis, a motive, or, to say the least, a point of view. The modern biographer rightly discards the commemorative or the didactic motive; the "spirit of the age" will have none of these things. It insists on absolute detachment from ethical or sentimental considerations, and this detachment becomes in itself the point of view, and tends all too readily to produce the aloof, the patronising, or at best the affectionately satirical. The problem which the biographer of the twentieth century has to solve is therefore that of combining the maximum of scientific material with the perfection of literary form. The problem has not, as yet, presented itself in an extreme shape, since the modern interest in biography is still only partially and incompletely scientific. But the difficulty has arisen. So long ago as 1881 Froude, in endeavouring to be impartial, became detached, and as he stood on one side watching the human frailties of the Carlyles, the smile of satire framed itself at moments on his lips. But we have advanced since Froude. The public now demand that the vast and various sea of human experience be put before them in a portable form. Sir Edmund Gosse, greatly daring, let down a bucket and gave us an enthralling analysis of the result; Mr. Strachey, on the other hand, took us aside and showed us, from a distance, beauties and verities which no one had remarked before.

Sir Edmund Gosse, for his part, had long been an expert both in the theory and practice of biography.

Sir Edmund Gosse. The article which he contributed on the subject to the *Encyclopædia Britannica* is a lucid exposition of what, in effect, is "pure" biography. For him biography is "the faithful portrait of a soul in its adventures through life." For him again "the peculiar curiosity which legitimate biography satisfies is essentially a modern thing, and presupposes our observation of life not unduly clouded by moral passion or prejudice." He lays no stress upon the literary element in biography. He would contend, I presume, that the essential element in biography is actuality, individuality; that the form of a biography is less important than its content. Here I agree. It is strange, however, that the author of *Father and Son*, which I consider to be the most "literary" biography in the English language, should not have grappled more closely with this problem of content *versus* form. For it is on the rocks of this problem that pure biography is doomed to split. In his other biographies Sir Edmund Gosse has relieved the pressure of facts, the explosive force of the scientific element, by the safety-valve of innuendo. He hints. This is all very well, and has enabled him to produce several highly graceful biographies and portraits in which, while not denying truth, he allows the extreme pressure of truth to evaporate and to escape. These works will for long remain as models of grace and dexterity, but they will not live as models of biography. Sir Edmund Gosse as a biographer will be judged by *Father and Son*. For to this work he brought great courage, great originality, and consummate literary art.

Consider, in the first place, his courage. A combination of circumstances had given him the privilege of witnessing, in a tragically concentrated form, the clash between the age of belief and the age of reason, the death struggle of Puritanism in its battle with science. He felt impelled to place on record his observation of that tragedy. It happened, however, that the struggle as he witnessed it had taken an acutely personal form, had resolved itself into the clash between his own temperament and that of his father. The full flow of convention, disguised as "good taste," ran counter to his purpose: yet he knew that his book was necessary, that it would do enormous good. He persisted, and by his persistence not only gave posterity a masterpiece, but won a signal victory for intellectual liberty. Let it not, moreover, be supposed that public opinion in 1907 was prepared for the shock occasioned by *Father and Son*. Victorianism only died in 1921. So late as 1911 we find Sir Sidney Lee speaking of the function and ethics of biography in a fully nineteenth-century spirit. Biography, for him, was essentially commemorative: it must be serious, it must possess a quality "which stirs and firmly holds the attention of the earnest-minded"; while aiming at "the truthful transmission of personality," it must deal with exploits as well as character, it must deal with important people. "Character," writes Sir Sidney, "which does not translate itself into exploit is for

(sidenote: "Father and Son" (1907).)

the biographer a mere phantasm"; or again, "the life of a nonentity or a mediocrity, however skilfully contrived, conflicts with primary biographic principles." [1]

It was in disregarding superstitions such as these that Sir Edmund Gosse demonstrated his originality. He set out, not to write a life, but to present "a genuine slice of life." The character of Philip Henry Gosse is displayed not through his zoological exploits, but in his domestic behaviour over a period of some twenty years. We have no record of the early struggles at Carbonear, in Canada, or in Alabama; we have but slight references to the happy Jamaica period; we are told nothing of the final period from 1870 to 1888. The book is not, therefore, a conventional biography; still less is it an autobiography. It is something entirely original; it is a triumphant experiment in a new formula; it is a clinical examination of states of mind over a detached and limited period. From one point of view the book is "a diagnosis of a dying Puritanism." From another point of view it is "a study of the development of moral and intellectual ideas during the progress of infancy." Yet it is far more than this. Underlying the story is a conflict of the utmost intensity. We have the clash of wills; the

[1] Sir Sidney Lee, Leslie Stephen Lecture, 1911.

constant hidden presence of a malignant deity; the intellectual blindness with which the father is afflicted and which impels him to the destruction of his own dearest hopes. There is all the apparatus of a Greek tragedy, and yet this tragic element is implicit only; it is never expressed. Sir Edmund Gosse's detachment from the tragedy in which he was so closely implicated is indeed amazing. He writes of it gently, humorously, ironically, pathetically; he is never sentimental, never angry, never intense. The texture of the book is uniform and soothing, like that of the finest velvet; anl yet, essentially, the book is scientific. We are shown a curious and indeed singular specimen of human character; this specimen is beautifully prepared for us and all irrelevant material is cleared away; we are provided with an easy-chair, and the softest cushions are afforded for our backs; the microscope is there ready to hand; and, thus accommodated, thus reclining, we listen to that soft and brilliant exposition. It does not last a moment longer than is necessary; it has all been tremendously interesting, and instructive too, and Sir Edmund through it all has been so wise, so witty, and so nice. Do we have a slight reaction? Do we feel, on looking back, that the Eumenides have, for the occasion, been dressed in sun-bonnets? Such reactions are not very enlightened and are not permanent. The permanent impression left by *Father and Son* is that of a masterpiece in which, by consummate power of selection, the author has been able to combine the maximum of scientific interest with the maximum of literary form.

Sir Edmund Gosse achieved his synthesis by processes of exclusion. Not only did he reject all such material as was irrelevant to his immediate purpose, but he rejected forty-eight years of his father's span of life. He thus limited his field of inquiry both in time and space, and was able to reduce his scientific investigation to manageable proportions. His father throughout the book remains fixed and rigid. Such development as occurs, occurs in the psychology of the observer, not in that of his subject. By this means the scientific interest is enormously enhanced, for it is through autobiography, and not through biography, that the development of character can most convincingly be conveyed. Mr. Strachey, in composing his *Queen Victoria*, could benefit by no such simplification. The mass of his material was overwhelming. He was faced with eighty-one solid years, and each one of these years was crowded with intricate and important events directly relevant to his subject. He was faced with innumerable secondary characters,

Mr. Lytton Strachey.

most of whom were so interesting in themselves as to distract attention from the central figure. He was faced with vast national movements, with vital developments in imperial, foreign, and domestic policy, with far-reaching changes in the industrial and social condition of England, with intricate modifications in the constitution, with obscure shapings of the national temperament, with all those hidden forces which within those eighty years completely altered the structure of the civilised world. To compress all this within some three hundred pages; to mould this vast material into a synthetic form; to convey not merely unity of impression but a convincing sense of scientific reality; to maintain throughout an attitude of detachment; to preserve the exquisite poise and balance of sustained and gentle irony, and to secure these objects with no apparent effort; to produce a book in which there is no trace of artificiality or strain—this, in all certainty, is an achievement which required the very highest gifts of intellect and imagination. Mr. Strachey, inevitably, has his point of view; and it is his point of view which dictates his method. Already in *Eminent Victorians* (1918) he had attacked the complacent credulity of the nineteenth century, and had exposed the several legends with which that objective age had flattered its own self-esteem. His criticism, however, was not merely destructive. He exposed, it is true, the worldliness of Manning, the harsh muddle-headedness of Arnold, the ill-temper of Florence Nightingale, the eccentricity of Gordon. Everybody was delighted and amused, but when they had recovered from their amusement they realised that behind it all lay something far more serious and important—a fervent belief, for instance, in intellectual honesty; an almost revivalist dislike of the second-hand, the complacent, or the conventional; a derisive contempt for emotional opinions; a calm conviction that thought and reason are in fact the most important elements in human nature; a respect, ultimately, for man's unconquerable mind. It is in directions such as these that Mr. Strachey has moulded the spirit of his age.

It was thus from the purely intellectual standpoint that Mr. Strachey approached the alarming problem of *Queen Victoria*. His intense intellectual honesty did not allow him to pretend that the events of those eighty years were explicable by any formula. He was not one of those who readily attribute the complex interaction of events to any divine or even human agency. He knew that life was largely inexplicable and fortuitous, that human actions are governed by chance more often than by will, by emo-

"Queen Victoria" (1921).

tion or instinct more often than by reason; he knew that public affairs are in general but a series of improvisations and expedients. His book, therefore, is primarily a criticism of life. It is secondarily a scientific examination of temperament, an attempt to estimate the effect of very exceptional experience upon a character which, although distinctive, was not intrinsically exceptional. It is this psychological motive, this psychological point of view, which gives the book its unity. The several minor figures—Baroness Lehzen, King Leopold, the Duchess of Kent, Melbourne, Prince Albert, Palmerston, Mr. Gladstone, Disraeli—are all introduced in so far only as they affect or illustrate Victoria's temperament. Public events—the Hastings scandal, the bedchamber question, the prerogative of the Crown, chartism, foreign politics, India, Ireland, the Empire—are all subordinated to the main psychological purpose, are introduced or explained only so far as is necessary to the elucidation of the central personality. A similar consistency of intention dictates the actual construction of the book, more than two-thirds being devoted to the long processes by which the character of Victoria was formed, and the remaining third dealing with her life after her character had crystallised. By thus concentrating his attention upon internal development rather than upon external events, Mr. Strachey was able to subdue his material and to allow himself full scope for the display of his own literary powers. The delicacy and precision of these powers can only properly be appreciated by those people who have endeavoured, and failed, to imitate them. We have all benefited enormously by Mr. Strachey's method; there is no reason why, if we are sufficiently intelligent, we should not share his point of view. It is a pity, however, that so many people should wish to imitate his style. It is unfortunate, indeed, that Mr. Strachey's sceptical detachment, his ironical use and juxtaposition of material, should have led to stylistic imitation. It all seems so easy until you attempt it, and it is then only that you realise that, compared with the amazing dexterity of Mr. Strachey, the fingers of his imitators are but thumbs. The more modest of us have, I observe, already abandoned our ungainly mimicry in despair; others, however, still persist, and this exquisitely delicate medium is rapidly becoming vulgarised. It is to be hoped that this imitation will cease.

Mr. Strachey, with all his virtues, does not finally solve the problem of the relation of biography to science on the one hand and to literature on the other. I am second to none in my admiration of *Queen Victoria*, but I cannot call it a "pure" biography. I have decried hagiology; I have indicated that Izaak Walton, in spite of his great literary merits, fails as a biographer because he is dominated by his own point of view. But have I not just been arguing that the constructive excellence of *Queen Victoria* is to be attributed to the fact that Mr. Strachey also had a point of view? The question is not whether Mr. Strachey's attitude is better or worse than that of Walton. The point is, firstly, that they both work on a personal thesis; and secondly, that any personal thesis on the part of the biographer is destructive of "pure" biography. Boswell had no thesis, nor had Lockhart: they worked wholly on the inductive method, and their literary skill was manifested solely in the arrangement and presentation of their specimens; they neither propounded nor implied a theory; they merely, with the requisite degree of taste and selection, furnished facts. Their facts, although extensive, were limited by the taste of their age. Their contemporaries did not expect, much less did they insist upon, an accumulation of "scientific" detail. It was physically possible for them to mould their facts into tolerable form, to compress them into some adequately convenient shape, without being obliged to employ any external aids to synthesis. Today, however, the reading public expect the biographer to regard all ascertainable fact as within his province: the material thereby collected becomes too enormous to be rendered as a whole; ordinary arrangement is of little avail, and some external aids to synthesis are essential. Sir Edmund Gosse coped with the problem by taking a section of the facts and examining that section in detail; Mr. Strachey coped with the problem by taking an aspect of the facts and examining that aspect from the psychological point of view. By these methods they both succeeded in producing first-class literature, but they did not succeed in producing "pure" biography.

What are the implications of all this? I would suggest, in the first place, that the scientific interest in biography is hostile to, and will in the end prove destructive of, the literary interest. The former will insist not only on the facts, but on all the facts; the latter demands a partial or artificial representation of facts. The scientific interest, as it develops, will become insatiable; no synthetic power, no genius for representation, will be able to keep the pace. I foresee, therefore, a divergence between the two interests. Scientific biography will become specialised and technical. There will be biographies in which psychological development will be traced in all its

The future of biography.

intricacy and in a manner comprehensible only to the experts; there will be biographies examining the influence of heredity—biographies founded on Galton, on Lombroso, on Havelock Ellis, on Freud; there will be medical biographies—studies of the influence on character of the endocrine glands, studies of internal secretions; there will be sociological biographies, economic biographies, æsthetic biographies, philosophical biographies. These will doubtless be interesting and instructive, but the emphasis which will be thrown on the analytical or scientific aspect will inevitably lessen the literary effort applied to their composition. The more that biography becomes a branch of science the less will it become a branch of literature.

The literary element will, of course, persist, but it will be driven into other directions. We may have some good satirical biographies, we may even have invective: I can well envisage the biography of hate. We shall have many sentimental biographies, a few idylls, a pastoral or an eclogue now and then. By some rare accident a man of talent may write a good inductive biography of some arresting personality with whom he has been intimate. But in general literary biography will, I suppose, wander off into the imaginative, leaving the strident streets of science for the open fields of fiction. The biographical form will be given to fiction, the fictional form will be given to biography. When this happens "pure" biography, as a branch of literature, will have ceased to exist.

Between these two extremes, between science and fiction, "professional" biography will, of course, pursue its way. There will be a constant supply of those ready-made biographies which the journeymen of letters provide for the library public. The taste for such works is now well established and universal. Between 1900 and 1915 alone some five hundred biographies were published annually in Great Britain. We shall continue to have second-rate reconstructional biographies, "life-and-times" biographies, biographies of gallantry and adventure, lives of the obscure, the intemperate, and the good. We shall have floods of memoirs and diaries, oceans of reprints and cheap editions, torrents of "men of action" and "men of science." We shall also, I am glad to say, have the two-volume obituary biography, the official "life," the standard book of reference. Such works, the aftermath of eminence, have been unjustly derided. They are inevitable, they are useful, they are frequently well written. It is seldom that they fall below the high standard set by such books as Trevelyan's *Macaulay* or Morley's *Gladstone*, and at moments, even, their uniform and solid excellence is illumined by some flash of brilliant synthesis, such as Mr. Churchill's *Life* of his father, or diversified by some unpretentious and charming volume, such as Mr. Charteris' recent *Life of Sargent*. Their fault, of course, is that they are admittedly commemorative; frequently they are not even spontaneous. An eminent man dies and his executors seek for some "suitable" biographer among his friends. The impulse comes from outside, and is to that extent artificial. It is only rarely that the biographer thus chosen can approach his work with the zest and the independence essential to his task.

To what, therefore, does this examination lead? I started by defining biography as "the history of the lives of individual men as a branch of literature." Have I abandoned this definition or have I added to it? I have insisted throughout on the three elements of truth, individuality, and art, and I have contended that biography cannot be "pure" biography unless all these three elements be combined. I have traced the evolution of truth and individuality from the fifth to the twentieth century, and I have implied that when they reach their zenith and combine in the form of scientific psychology, they destroy the third of my essential elements, they put an end to

The end of "pure" biography.

"pure" biography as a branch of literature. I believe this to be true. I believe that the three essential elements cannot again be combined in their proper proportions, that we shall not have another Boswell or another Lockhart. Nor do I see that this is of any very essential importance. We shall have franker and fuller autobiographies than we have yet been accorded, and this in itself will compensate for the separation of literature from "pure" biography. The literary element in "pure" biography was always the least important of the three; the scientific biography will demand but a minimum of literary representation; and literature, by devoting itself to "impure" or applied biography, may well discover a new scope, an unexplored method of conveying human experience.